INTEGRATING EXTREMES

"With great skill, Lisa focuses our attention on how the autonomic nervous system is at the center of our work with our young ones. She translates the science into practical ways we can be with ourselves and with our clients to foster healing the extreme emotions that are touched in play. With humor and compassion, Lisa offers a way through these challenging times. A very helpful read for any play therapist."

—BONNIE BADENOCH, PhD, LMFT,
Author of *Being a Brain-Wise Therapist*

"This groundbreaking book brings to light the scientific fact that it isn't about the child's behavior; it's about the child's regulation—as well as the therapist's regulation. This book will be an invaluable resource that finally gives therapists permission to get back to playing with children instead of "therapizing" them.

—HEATHER T. FORBES, LCSW, Author of *Beyond Consequences, Logic, and Control: A Love-Based Approach to Helping Attachment-Challenged Children with Severe Behaviors, Volumes 1 and 2; Help for Billy: A Beyond Consequences Approach to Helping Challenging Children in the Classroom; Dare to Love: The Art of Merging Science and Love into Parenting Children with Difficult Behaviors.*

"Finally a book that shows Therapists, School Counselors, Social Workers, and First Responders how to simultaneously keep themselves healthy while effectively helping children to work through trauma and learn to regulate their nervous systems! This book offers a promising therapeutic approach that's grounded in neurobiological processes allowing therapists to facilitate true emotional healing in the children they treat and also experience healing themselves."

—KATHRYN CLARKE, LPC, RPT-S, Registered Play Therapy Supervisor, Certified Synergetic Play Therapy Supervisor

"This powerful and dynamic book is clear, concise and chockfull of valuable information for anyone wishing to learn to work therapeutically with children and take care of themselves at the same time."

—SUSAN FRIEDMANN, CSP, International Bestselling Author of *Riches in Niches: How to Make it BIG in a small Market*

INTEGRATING EXTREMES

*Aggression and Death
in the Playroom*

LISA DION, LPC, RPT-S

Aviva Publising

New York

Library of Congress Control Number: 2015919286

ISBN: 978-1-943164-38-7

Interior Illustrations: Krista Reinhardt-Ruprecht
Cover and Interior Design: AuthorSupport.com

This book is dedicated to all my child clients, my students and my own daughter, Avery, for teaching me that the best way to navigate challenging situations is to be yourself and take deep breaths.

Contents

ACKNOWLEDGMENTS

To all my students over the years who kept asking me to write this book, it was your vulnerability with your stories and your belief in me that inspired me to write this book for you.

This book would not have happened without the help of my loved ones, my friends, and the enormous support system that believed in me more than I believed in myself at times. Writing this book required me to face my own fears in order to discover my authentic voice. It also required me to embody all of the teachings that I present in this book. I am so grateful for the transformation that has occurred within me as a result.

A special "thank you" goes to the following people:

My family, especially my mom, Terri Terni, and my dad, Steve Terni, for your love and deep belief in me.

My daughter, Avery, for your unyielding patience and understanding while I spent hours writing. Thank you also for all the times that you told your friends and even strangers, "My mom is writing a book about sword-fighting!" because you were so excited and proud.

Jeremy Dion, for cheerleading me on and believing in my potential. Thank you for caring for our daughter and giving me the freedom to pursue my dreams.

My dear friends Enette Pauze and Jolina Karen, for helping me face my fears when I got stuck writing this book and needed some encouragement.

Bill Brakemeier, for strengthening me to go after my purpose and mission. I am grateful for your contribution to the making of this book.

My child clients, for swinging swords at me, handcuffing me, shooting me, yelling at me and working so hard to help me understand your world. This book is also for you.

Kathy Clarke, my "transition object," for your unwavering support and belief in the power of this work. Your belief in me and Synergetic Play Therapy has given me wings.

Steve Terni (my dad), Erin Rupert and Rebecca Terni, for helping transcribe, read and edit parts of the book. Your honest input was invaluable in the making of this book.

My mentor, Dr. John Demartini, for giving me permission to challenge my "shoulds" and for encouraging me to go for it in life.

Thank you also to Stephen Terni, my twin brother, for being with me every step of the way.

Krista Reinhardt-Ruprecht, for your inspiration and artistic talent with the illustrations. Thank you for adding such an important element to the book.

Jerry Dorris from AuthorSupport.com, for your creative design with the cover and inside of the book. Thank you for pulling the book together and helping my dream manifest into my hands.

Susan Friedmann from Aviva Publishing, for your publishing wisdom. Your guidance and support was invaluable.

Toni Robino and Doug Wagner of Windword Literary Services, for your editing and writing genius. This book would not have happened without you. Thank you for holding my hand through the journey of bringing this book to life.

FOREWORD

Finally, a voice of reason when it comes to working with traumatized children in play therapy! Lisa Dion explains the necessity of being present, authentic, and regulated when faced with the intensity that trauma presents in the play experience. *Integrating Extremes* embraces what every child's healing process needs: intensity, connection, attunement, authenticity, and openness.

Lisa Dion beautifully integrates the science of affect dysregulation into the art of healing while simultaneously giving practical and clear direction for therapists to use in their work with children. She makes the science easy to understand and reinforces its application with some of her own experiences in working with children. The integration of her stories throughout this book keeps the reader's attention and makes for an interesting read.

Lisa Dion explains spot on how the clinician must be comfortable with high states of arousal and that this is now the new "normal" when working with traumatized children. She poignantly makes the case that clinicians must be one with the child in order to fully help a child to integrate his or her trauma. Trauma in real life isn't sugarcoated for children, and thus we can no longer attempt to sugarcoat it for children in therapy. A child's fear and pain need to be released in their fullest and most raw form, which requires us to throw out some of the traditional and ridiculous "rules of therapy" that have previously gotten in the way of our children's healing.

Additionally, Lisa Dion emphasizes the challenges that intense play presents to the therapist's own regulation. Traditional training has failed to acknowledge how high-intensity play will ultimately wake up a therapist's own dormant trauma—at a very personal level. The author boldly makes the point that when the therapist's own unfinished business rises to the surface and activates his or her nervous systems, it is the therapist's responsibility to be aware of such increases in arousal. No longer can this be either consciously or subconsciously projected back onto a child.

Lisa Dion's advice to stop fixing the child but to stay attuned to the child's own inherent healing process is exactly on target. We must trust that children know exactly what they need. It takes following the child's lead and dancing with whatever the child's imagination creates in each interaction to accomplish this goal.

This groundbreaking book brings to light the scientific fact that it isn't about the child's behavior; it's about the child's regulation—as well as the therapist's regulation. This book will be an invaluable resource that finally gives therapists permission to get back to playing with children instead of "therapizing" them.

Heather T. Forbes, LCSW
Author: *Beyond Consequences, Logic, and Control: A Love-Based Approach to Helping Attachment-Challenged Children with Severe Behaviors, Volumes 1 and 2; Help for Billy: A Beyond Consequences Approach to Helping Challenging Children in the Classroom; Dare to Love: The Art of Merging Science and Love into Parenting Children with Difficult Behaviors.*

CHAPTER 1

Aggression and Death in the Playroom

The swords were flying. I was dodging and blocking the blows, but I was barely able to keep up with this five-year-old's swings. I was beginning to feel overwhelmed. In this whirlwind of energy, all my brain was registering was, "Protect myself, protect myself, protect myself." Seconds later, I felt something hard hit my head. The pain brought me back to the moment, and I immediately knew it wasn't the sword he was using. Without the ability to block out an authentic response,

1

I sank to the floor with tears welling in my eyes and blurted out, "I'm scared." This little boy, who was a witness and victim of domestic violence, looked into my eyes, put down his weapons and crawled into my lap. He began to gently rock back and forth, saying, "Me, too. Me, too." In that moment, I finally understood his world. I felt it at my core.

In my session with Carlos, when the sense of overwhelm got to be too much, I lost my ability to stay present. I emotionally flooded and checked out. It was the blow to my head that brought me back. The shock and pain was so intense that I wasn't able to block out my authentic response, and when Carlos saw me sink to the floor with tears in my eyes, he knew that I was being real and that I understood his fear.

Through my roles as a supervisor and teacher, I've heard hundreds of therapists' stories about their confusion and emotional struggles regarding aggressive play. They've also told me about the physical pain they've endured trying to help some of their child clients. I've heard stories of sessions filled with sword fights, being killed and left to die, being handcuffed and locked away, explosions, dismemberment, injured babies, sexual intrusion and physical abuse. I've listened to therapists questioning their role in the playroom, whether or not they want to be play therapists, and more important, questioning themselves. *I get it.* I've struggled with these dilemmas, too.

When I first became a play therapist, I discovered that I had the capacity to work with high levels of trauma, but no one taught me how to avoid absorbing the high level of intense energy. After sessions, I often felt drained, tired and agitated. But I also saw that the children I was working with were transforming. I wanted to help them heal, but I didn't want to be a punching bag or a trauma trash can. Whether I was watching a child play aggressively or I was experiencing the aggression directly, the energy was so jarring to my nervous system that I knew I had to change something or I'd be at major risk for compassion fatigue, burnout or injury.

Moments of truth, like the one that came when I was hit in the head while playing with Carlos, together with the messages I got from listening to my body, inspired my journey to discover how to help children heal by using methods that support them and myself as their therapist. Thanks to the thousands of children I've worked with and the therapists who have so courageously shared their struggles with me, I have a new perspective on aggression and death play that I'll share with you throughout this book.

A PROMISING NEW PARADIGM

Integrating Extremes introduces an understanding of aggression and death from the perspective of the nervous system. When we look at aggression and death from this perspective, we begin to understand that children's biology is attempting to integrate their hyper (sympathetic) and hypo (parasympathetic) aroused states as they work through their traumatic memories and sensations. This will be explored in full detail in Chapter 2. This perspective also highlights the need for the therapist to practice self-regulation and authentic expression, which will be discussed in Chapters 3 and 5. For now, regulation means the ability to manage the physical sensations and emotions in your body. This chapter outlines some basic ideas that will be helpful as you read the rest of the book. It will also explain why I believe a new paradigm is so necessary, the importance of aggression and death in the playroom and how to choose aggressive toys for your playroom. With that foundation, I will then share stories and principles throughout the book showing you how you can work with aggression and death play.

This book is for any therapist, social worker, teacher or caregiver who is asked to play with a child at a high level of intensity or witnesses a child playing with high intensity. Navigating swords fights, being handcuffed and shot and watching violent play while staying present and facilitating the intensity is an art. Often, we're taken right to the edge of our capacity to hold the energy in the playroom and we lose ourselves for a moment (or longer). This book presents a paradigm that's a way back to yourself so that you can help children heal at profound levels and access the most authentic parts of yourself in the process. It's the art of learning how to be deeply authentic in the playroom while facilitating a deep level of healing for the child.

Most of us decided to become play therapists because we have a sincere desire to help children. We're led by a yearning to help children heal. We didn't choose this profession to get physically or emotional hurt, but sometimes we do. The new paradigm I'm presenting is a framework for helping us to authentically work with the intensity of aggression and death play without getting hurt or causing our nervous systems to start shutting down in response to the intensity.

SOMETIMES PLAY THERAPY ISN'T ENOUGH

In the cases of many of the children you work with, the information I'm sharing will be enough to help you support them during your play therapy sessions. You'll be able to use this framework to help them integrate their traumatic experiences while keeping yourself safe and sane. In other cases, it will be a piece of the puzzle. Play therapy isn't enough for some children. Children who have experienced highly traumatic events often need additional support such as occupational therapy, speech therapy, academic support or intensive family play therapy. The caregivers of these children often need intensive parenting support. Whenever possible, make sure you're working with the family and caregivers to give them the tools and supports they need, because they also need our help along this journey. Use your best clinical judgment to know when you need to bring in additional help and support.

SYNERGETIC PLAY THERAPY

The foundation for the paradigm I'm presenting is founded in Synergetic Play Therapy— the type of therapy I practice and teach. I draw from my own stories in the playroom and the principles of this model to help us explore what's happening between the therapist and the child during aggression and death play. You don't need to be a Synergetic Play therapist or to have studied this model of play therapy to understand the concepts in this book. Synergetic Play Therapy is a model of therapy based on nervous-system regulation and neuroscience, attunement, mindfulness and therapist authenticity.

These are essential components of making aggression and death play deeply therapeutic and transformative. Although Synergetic Play Therapy is called a model of play therapy, it's actually a way of being in relationship with self and other. It's an all-encompassing paradigm that can be applied to any facet of life, and subsequently any model of play therapy can be applied to it or vice versa. Use the information in this book to deepen the type of play therapy you do. The information will help you develop a greater understanding of yourself in the playroom and will show you how to facilitate aggression and death play in a way that truly allows healing to occur for the child and for you. (For more information on this model, visit synergeticplaytherapy.com.)

THE PLAYROOM IS THE PERFECT PLACE FOR AGGRESSION AND DEATH

In our culture, aggression tends to be viewed as a no-no. When a child starts to play aggressively in a session, we can get caught up in trying to decide if we should let it play out or stop it. *Is this okay? Should I allow this? If we play like this, are they going to play like this with their friends? Am I promoting aggression? Should I be teaching social norms such as "Hitting is not appropriate"?* These are the questions I hear every time I teach a seminar on working with aggression. They speak to the confusion that often arises inside us. Without understanding what the aggression actually means or how to work with it, we often default to what we think is the *right* thing to do, which may not be the most therapeutic thing.

The playroom is the child's safe and contained place for exploring their feelings, memories and body sensations. It's the place where they get to do, say and move in ways that may not be acceptable outside the playroom. Having this understanding helps us to consider the value of aggressive play. It leads us to ask ourselves, "Is this a social skills class or a therapy session?" If it is indeed a social skills class or the focus of the session is on teaching the child appropriate rules for interacting with others, a different approach toward the aggression might be appropriate. But if you're doing one-on-one trauma work with a child, it's absolutely necessary for the child to be able to explore his or her aggression because that's how children can learn about it and ultimately learn how to regulate through it. The beautiful thing is that as we help our child clients explore their aggressive urges in ways that promote integration, we're also teaching them how to be in relationship with others.

When we're supporting a child in working through traumatic experiences, we have to be willing to let in any aspect of the trauma that needs to enter the room so that the child can work through it with our help. Some therapists worry that allowing the aggressive play inside the playroom might promote or intensify aggression elsewhere; the concern is that we might be giving the child permission to aggressively play with others. *Integrating Extremes* offers ways to make exploring aggression therapeutic without promoting it outside the playroom. You'll learn about the biology behind aggression and death play, and you'll also learn how to regulate through the intensity and model those techniques to your clients.

Although this book focuses on the intensity that arises with aggression and death in the playroom, all children's biology is attempting to integrate their hyper and hypo aroused states as they play. So what you learn in this book will help you with all your clients, not just the challenging ones.

PLAYING WITH EXTREME ENERGY

As therapists, we're engaged in aggression and death play in two primary ways. One is dramatic play that we're actively participating in. It might involve a sword fight, a gunfight, being handcuffed and arrested, being injured or being killed. The other way is when we're in the role of the observer. In this play, we watch as the child wages a massive war in the sand tray, creates intense images through art, stacks blocks and kicks them down, makes stuffed toys pummel each other or leaves wounded dolls alone and neglected. Whether we're participating in or watching this type of play, it's intense because it activates both the hyper (sympathetic) and hypo (parasympathetic) aroused states of our nervous system. Both extremes are uncomfortable, so our gut reaction is to avoid them.

It's normal for therapists to be somewhat uncomfortable with extreme energy, especially if we don't know what to do with it or what it means. Let's be honest—it can be scary! If we have negative associations in our personal history that remotely resemble or remind us of that energy, it's even scarier and our protective patterns will probably come into play. This is normal and will happen. Facilitating aggression and death in the playroom isn't about avoiding or trying to prevent the intensity from happening—it's about learning how to be with yourself and your experience so that you can move toward what you're experiencing, which creates the opportunity to change your own neural wiring and protective patterns. Once you learn how to stay connected to yourself in the midst of the fear, you can manage and integrate what you're experiencing.

Most play therapists are not well-educated in how to make

aggression and death play therapeutic. Since we're not superhuman, this level of intensity can affect our lives outside of playroom. Before I had an understanding of neurobiology or knew how to use regulation in a therapy session, I had many sessions where I walked out at the end thinking, "I just got emotionally beat up and shut down for forty-five minutes!" At times, I even took it personally and felt angry with the child. Often my agitation would spill over into other areas of my life, leaving me and my loved ones feeling frustrated and overwhelmed.

I realized that we have to work with our experience or we'll spend our time shut down or overwhelmed, putting ourselves at risk for burnout and compassion fatigue. We might start having nightmares, snap at our loved ones or find it difficult not to think about our clients when we aren't at the office. Another common reaction is to become desensitized or emotionally numb. We might experience signs or symptoms of depression or become very analytical, obsessively trying to figure out what happened to certain kids to distract ourselves from what we're feeling. These are all symptoms of a dys-regulated nervous system, meaning our nervous system is feeling out of whack. (In Chapter 2, I explain the symptoms of a dys-regulated nervous system in detail.)

YOU ARE NOT ALONE

If you've felt overwhelmed, shut down, physically exhausted, sleep-deprived and dreaded seeing certain clients, you're not alone. Have you ever looked at your schedule and thought, "Oh, no! I have to see Johnny at four o'clock," as you feel the intensity or exhaustion of the last session creep into your body? If so, you know what I'm talking about. I want you to know that this is all common and normal. I have yet to meet a play therapist who didn't struggle with this at some point. The reason these symptoms are normal is that our brains are wired to perceive aggression and death as a potential threat because instinctually we know we might not be safe. It's no wonder then that we cringe a little when a client starts racing around the room shooting us, throwing toys at us, leaving us to die or creating aggressive play for us to observe.

CHOOSING TOYS FOR TRAUMA WORK

Over the years, I've seen a wide range of aggressive toys in the playroom: plastic knives, handcuffs, bop bags, all types of swords and everything from three-inch water guns to plastic machine guns that look and sound real. But I haven't seen a correlation between what the toys look like and the depth that children will go to in their work with toys. I've seen kids resist going deeper for other reasons, but it's never been about the toys themselves.

Children will use whatever is available to do their work. I suggest that therapists have aggressive toys to help kids work through their traumatic memories and emotions, but I don't think the toys have to look real. For example, children will use a three-inch fluorescent water gun the same way they'll use a toy that looks like a real machine gun. (For the water gun, make sure to fill the hole with Play-Doh and take out the stopper unless you really want it to be used as a water gun!) Using toys that don't look like real weapons helps to keep the aggression inside the playroom because the emphasis is on facilitation and integration of the aggressive energy as opposed to shooting the therapist with a gun that looks real.

When you're thinking about which toys to have in your playroom, consider ones that do the job but don't necessarily resemble the real thing. For example, I've discovered that the best sword is a pool noodle cut in half to make a pair. They're cheap, they don't bend like most play swords and they don't hurt when they hit you. Set the pool-noodle swords next to a shield and children will know exactly what to do with them. Since they don't look like swords, they can also be used in other ways.

Carefully considering the types of aggressive toys you have in the playroom will also help you to work more effectively with the children's parents and caregivers. Most parents, at some point or another, will see the playroom, and parents who are uncomfortable with aggression will express fear or non-acceptance of the aggressive toys you have. Toys that look less threatening promote the healing without triggering the parents' fear response. If you have parents who express concern about the aggressive toys, you have the option to take those toys out. Children will do their work regardless of whether a particular toy is available or not. If they need to work on aggression, they'll turn a marker into a knife, make a gun out of Legos or use their forefinger and thumb to shoot you. You can also choose to educate the parents on the importance of aggressive play in the play therapy process.

Now that we've covered some basics, grab your swords, shields and helmets as we jump into exploring aggression and death in the playroom. In the next chapter, you'll find out why kids need to play out aggression and death from the perspective of human biology and the nervous system. And you'll learn why it's so easy to become dys-regulated and why it's so important to self-regulate as we experience or observe aggression and death in the playroom. Once you learn how to regulate, it will be easier for you to work with the aggression and intensity your clients bring into the room without getting overwhelmed, burning out or shutting down.

We all get dys-regulated every day, not because there's something wrong with us but because we're human. The remedy is to learn how to get ourselves back into a regulated state every time our nervous system gets dys-regulated. With practice, your nervous system will become more resilient, you'll become dys-regulated less frequently, and when you do, you'll be able to breathe through it and bounce back faster.

CHAPTER 1 KEY POINTS

- When we watch a child play aggressively or experience the aggression directly, the energy is so jarring to our nervous systems that we have to change something or we'll be at major risk for compassion fatigue, burnout or injury.

- When we look at aggression and death from the perspective of the nervous system, we understand that children's biology is attempting to integrate their hyper (sympathetic) and hypo (parasympathetic) aroused states as they work through their traumatic memories and sensations.

- We can authentically work with the intensity of aggression and death play without getting hurt or causing our own nervous systems to start to shut down in response to the intensity.

- Children who have experienced highly traumatic events in their lives often need additional support such as occupational therapy, speech therapy, academic support and intensive family play therapy. Parents need support, too.

- Synergetic Play Therapy is a model of therapy based on nervous-system regulation and neuroscience, attunement, mindfulness and therapist authenticity. It's an all-encompassing paradigm that can be applied to any facet of life, and subsequently any model of play therapy can be applied to it or vice versa.

- Without understanding what the aggression actually means or how to work with it, we will often default to what we think is the *right* thing to do, which may not be the most therapeutic thing.

- The playroom is the child's safe and contained place for exploring his or her feelings, memories and body sensations.

- When we're doing one-on-one trauma work with a child, it is absolutely necessary for the child to be able to explore his or her aggression because that's how children can learn about it and ultimately learn how to regulate through it. We have to be willing to let in any aspect of the trauma that needs to enter the room so that the child can work through it with our help.

- It's normal for therapists to be somewhat uncomfortable with extreme energy, especially if we don't know what to do with it or what it means.

- Facilitating aggression and death in the playroom isn't about avoiding or trying to prevent the intensity from happening. It's about learning how to be present with our experience and ourselves so we can move into the experience and create the opportunity to change our neural wiring and protective patterns.

- Our brains are wired to perceive aggression and death as a potential threat because instinctually we know we might not be safe.

- Children will use whatever toy or object is available to do their work. There is no observable correlation between what the toys look like and the depth that children will go to in their work.

- Once we learn how to regulate, it's easier to work with the aggression and intensity that our clients bring into the room without getting overwhelmed, burning out or shutting down.

- With practice, our nervous systems become more resilient, we become dys-regulated less frequently, and when we do, we're able to breathe through it and bounce back faster.

CHAPTER 2

Exploring a New Perspective

"We use the relationship to allow our clients to re-experience dys-regulating affects in affectively tolerable doses in the context of a safe environment, so that overwhelming traumatic feelings can be regulated and integrated into the patient's emotional life." –Allan Shore[1]

Understanding how the brain and the nervous system process information gives us insight into why aggression and death play are necessary components of play therapy. Knowing how the brain and the nervous system interpret information and influence symptoms in the body helps us work with a child's behaviors and impulses that we might traditionally judge as "bad."

According to Joe Dispenza, author of Evolve Your Brain: The Science of Changing Your Mind, our brain processes four hundred billion bits of sensory data per second.[2] Our brains are constantly taking in and processing sensory data related to our external environment—what we see, smell, feel, hear and taste—as well as sensory data related to our internal environment—our hormone levels, glucose levels, heart rate and body temperature.

This is an extraordinary amount of information for our brains to integrate, and here's the *really* amazing part: We're consciously aware of only two thousand bits of it.[3] Pause for a moment and consider the relevance of that detail. If we're aware of less than 1 percent of all sensory data, the majority of what we experience isn't even on our conscious radar. We're not consciously aware of the vast majority of information we take in. We register it on an implicit level, which means that our body registers it but we're not mentally aware of it. The reason this is so significant is that in the playroom, many therapists feel so much more than they allow themselves to be consciously aware of. Whether your mind registers it or not, your body is aware of what's happening and is responding accordingly.

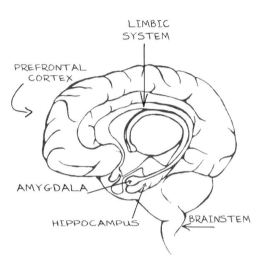

Once all this sensory data enters our brains, it makes its way up to the amygdala, situated in the limbic area of the brain. The amygdala plays a very important role—it's the part of the brain that determines whether the data it receives identifies a possible threat. It makes an immediate decision about whether a threat is or isn't present based on experience and knowledge. It's asking, "Have I seen this data before? Do I know anything about this data? Do I need to be scared? Do I need to protect myself? What do I know about this combination of sensory data?" If the amygdala decides there's a threat, it will send a signal to activate the autonomic nervous system telling it to respond.

Have you ever wondered why people in the same situation can have different responses to a traumatic event? Or how one child can have more symptoms than his or her siblings even though they were all raised in the same environment? Or how one adult can walk away from a tragic situation with little dysregulation and another walks away with PTSD symptoms? Trauma is entirely dependent on the *perception* of the event and whether we are able to integrate the sensory data.

OUR NERVOUS SYSTEM'S DEFINITION OF A THREAT

When we hear the word *threat,* we tend to think of something that's challenging our physical or emotional safety, but the amygdala's definition of a threat is much broader than that. In addition to scanning sensory data for what could be a physical or emotional threat, the brain is on alert for *the unknown.* The brain likes to know. It likes predictability.

Reflection:

Think of a time when you encountered the unknown. Maybe you were traveling and interacting with a culture that was completely foreign to you. Maybe you were eating at a restaurant and when the waiter set your plate in front of you, you couldn't quite tell what it was. Maybe you lost a job and woke up the next day not knowing what was going to happen next. If you mentally take yourself back to a moment when you've encountered the unknown, you'll recall that you paused for a second. That's a normal and necessary response.

When you think back about the particular "unknown" you recalled, you'll probably agree that it wasn't the unknown itself that was scary—it was the associations and memories about the possibilities of what could occur that were scary. Your brain is primed to pause when it perceives an unknown. It's your brain's way of saying, "Let's check this out just to make sure everything is safe."

Another threat or challenge the brain is scanning for is *incongruence in the environment.* Let's go back to the story I shared in Chapter 1. When I was sword-fighting with Carlos, I wasn't being congruent. I was role-playing, which is what I had been taught to do in my play therapy training. I wasn't giving myself permission to say out loud how I really felt when the sword was coming at me hard and fast. And I definitely wasn't regulating through it. I was just taking it, and as I was taking it, I was becoming less grounded. The result was that he kept amping it up. Why? Because I was incongruent. I was giving him mixed signals. My nonverbals were screaming that I was scared, but the rest of me was trying to stay cool and collected. I was part of the threat! He had to amp it up until he got an authentically congruent response from me.

THE PITFALLS OF 'SHOULD'

Have you ever noticed what happens to your body and emotions when someone "shoulds" you or you "should" yourself? Stop and think about it for a moment. What happens when you hear messages like "You *should* spend more time doing this" or "You *shouldn't* act like that"? What happens when you tell yourself, "I *shouldn't* feel that way or I *shouldn't* have said that"?

Reflection:

Think of a "should" that you've been saying to yourself recently. Take a deep breath and close your eyes. Say your "should" to yourself a few times and observe what happens in your body. If you observe closely, you'll notice that you probably experienced some degree of dys-regulation. Agitation, irritation, aggression, defensiveness, fatigue, depression, tightness and heaviness in the body, quickening of the heart rate, and hopelessness are all common experiences.

"*Shoulds*" are a challenge because they're perceived as a threat to our sense of self. Nobody likes to be told that they should be different from who they are. When we "should" ourselves, we're directly challenging our authentic self. We're denying who we are in the moment and not seeing our own wisdom. This can create an internal dilemma between who we are and who we think we should be. The result is that the autonomic nervous system becomes activated trying to handle the discrepancy.

The Four Threats:

1. Physical and emotional pain
2. The unknown
3. Incongruence in the environment
4. "Shoulds"

THE NERVOUS SYSTEM IN ACTION

The autonomic nervous system has two sides: a sympathetic branch for revving us up and a parasympathetic branch for slowing us down. The sympathetic branch is responsible for the fight-or-flight response, and the parasympathetic branch is responsible for the freeze-or-fall asleep response, also referred to as the freeze-or-faint response.

SYNERGETIC PLAY THERAPY™

Nervous System Symptoms of Regulation and Dys-regulation

All symptoms of dys-regulation arise out of mis-perceptions of the events in our lives. When we change our perceptions, we change the symptoms in our nervous system. It is wise to master the art of how to change our perceptions and how to manage the symptoms that arise in our bodies to help return us to a more regular state.

Hypo-arousal Symptoms- Excessive Parasympathetic Response- Freeze, Fall Asleep	Regulated Nervous System (Mindfulness/Attached to Self)	Hyper-arousal Symptoms- Excessive Sympathetic Response- Fight, Flight
Helplessness	Think logically	Increased heart rate
Inability to set boundaries	Think clearly	"Pounding" sensation in the head
Tired	Able to make conscious choices	Overwhelmed, Disorganized
Automatic obedience	Able to make eye contact	Habitual defensiveness
Appear life-less	Display a wide range of emotional expression	Aggression
Non-expressive	Feel "grounded"	Hyper-alertness
Numbing	Able to notice breath	Hyper-vigilance
Lack of motivation	Sleep Cycles Stable	Excessive Motoric Activity
Lethargic	Poised	Uncontrollable bouts of rage
Dulled capacity to feel significant events	Internal awareness of both mind and body	Highly irritable
Emotional constriction	"In the body"	Overwhelms others
Isolation/Depression	Able to communicate verbally in a clear manner	Anxious

Have you ever wondered why you have a fight-or-flight response instead of a freeze-or-fall asleep response or vice versa? Did you know there's a choice? It turns out that the branch we choose is based on our *perception* of the threat or challenge. If we perceive that we can do something about it, our sympathetic branch will have an excessive response and the fight-or-flight system will be activated. Our energy will travel from the core of our body to our arms, legs, feet and hands so we can fight or run. We can actually feel the energy in our hands and feet and we start moving. We also get a surge of energy to our face and head. This primal response makes our face flush, our jaws tense and our eyes widen to take in data. Our heart rate increases and we might feel a pounding sensation in our head. We're hyper-alert and hyper-vigilant and we become both defensive and aggressive. We might begin to feel overwhelmed and anxious, and it might be hard to stop moving. That's the essence of being hyper-aroused.

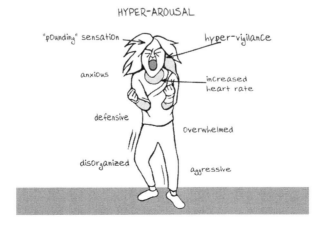

HYPER-AROUSAL

"pounding" sensation — hyper-vigilance — anxious — increased heart rate — defensive — overwhelmed — disorganized — aggressive

But what happens when we perceive the threat as overwhelming and believe we can't do anything about it? When we don't feel big enough, fast enough, loud enough, smart enough or strong enough to combat the threat, our nervous system begins to shut down, going into an excessive hypo-aroused response, and we freeze or feel sleepy. At an extreme level, we can dissociate and even faint. When the kids in our playroom are hypo-aroused, they often feel helpless and depressed and don't want to be seen. They can seem tired, with not much affect or expression. At extreme levels, they're almost ghost-like and robotic; the lack of energy in their extremities makes them numb. That's an attempt to stop the pain, but it leads to emotional constriction and feelings of isolation and depression. These children are shut down. They're in the room, but nobody's home. The same series of events happens for us when we have an excessive hypo-aroused response.

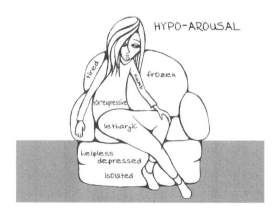

Our perception of the challenge or threat activates our nervous system into a hyper- or hypo-aroused response. When I was in the sword fight with Carlos, my brain was taking in a lot of sensory data. That data made its way to my amygdala, at which point it quickly assessed whether there was a possible threat. The decision was a definite "YES!" At that point, a signal was sent to activate my autonomic nervous system to do something about the perceived challenge.

At first my brain perceived that I could do something about it, so I had a hyper-aroused response and attempted to fight back. Since I was not regulating or having an authentic response and he began to speed up and intensify the swings coming at me, I started to believe I couldn't do anything about it and I began to check out in a hypo-aroused response. This all occurred within minutes and then—*bam*—I got hit in the head. To this day, I still have no idea what he hit me with.

Therapists who perceive threats as they deal with the intense aggression and death energy in the playroom for an extended period of time without regulating will probably begin to manifest signs of hypo-arousal. Our nervous systems can handle only so much.

NERVOUS SYSTEMS IN THERAPY

It's more common for children who are expressing excessive hyper-aroused symptoms to be referred to therapy, but we need to make sure we aren't forgetting about the hypoaroused children and educate parents and teachers about the need for these children to receive support. Sometimes these kids are overlooked because they're easy and compliant, but we need to keep in mind that they are in a hypo-aroused state, which means their perception is that the challenges are too big and they've already begun to shut down their emotional worlds. This is in contrast with the child who's acting out and therefore still believes he has a chance.

We all work with kids who have been diagnosed with or show signs of having a wide range of disorders, including oppositional defiant disorder, conduct disorder, anxiety disorder, bipolar disorder, post-traumatic stress, attention-deficit disorders, and depressive disorders. What's fascinating is to consider the idea that every symptom and diagnosis a child brings into therapy is the result of a dys-regulated nervous system, which means an excessive activation of the sympathetic (hyper aroused) or parasympathetic (hypo aroused) branches.

Maybe instead of diagnosing our kids with a disorder, the diagnosis needs to be "He's dys-regulated in an excessive hyper-aroused way" or "She's dys-regulated in an excessive hypo-aroused way." How would we approach our child clients in the playroom if we viewed them through this lens? How would this change the way we support parents and teachers when they're struggling with a child?

> *The child's symptoms are understood as symptoms of dys-regulated states of the nervous system. – Synergetic Play Therapy tenet*

Understanding the symptoms of the nervous system when a threat or challenge is perceived can give us insight into the child's perception of how big the challenge is. It also gives us information regarding our own perceptions when we begin to experience symptoms.

NERVOUS SYSTEMS IN AGGRESSION AND DEATH PLAY

Very simply put, aggression and death play are the symbolic forms of hyper-aroused and hypo-aroused states of the nervous system. As children begin to play, their associated memories and bodily sensations will arise. As a result, they'll begin to show signs of dys-regulation in their nervous systems as they attempt to work with the challenging information that's coming up for them. (Refer back to the nervous system chart on page 26 for a reminder of the symptoms.)

When the children or the play become aggressive and intense, it simply means that their nervous systems are moving into a highly activated sympathetic response. When death shows up in the playroom, as the therapist is lying there dead, the room is filled with the energy of a highly activated parasympathetic response. It's interesting to note that these two energies often show up in pairs in the playroom. In dramatic play, just at the moment that the aggressive energy has reached its peak as the child corners the therapist and shoots him (hyper-aroused), the therapist begins to die, lose power and become helpless (hypo-aroused). In observational play, the same is true. As the war in the sand tray reaches a high state of chaos and aggression (hyper-aroused), the soldiers under fire begin to die and many even fall over or disappear under the sand (hypo-aroused).

When we understand that aggression and death are the symbolic forms of the extreme arousal states of a child's nervous system, we can embrace a paradigm for healing based on nervous system regulation: All behavior, including aggression, is an attempt at regulation. Given that, our goal is to teach children how to regulate through their intense states of dys-regulation that arise when aggression and death enter the playroom, not to get rid of them. When we help children move toward their intense emotional states and sensations rather than move away from them, we're developing resiliency in the children while helping to re-pattern their nervous systems.

In the next chapter, we'll look at what regulation really means, and you'll learn the basics of regulating your nervous system.

CHAPTER 2 KEY POINTS

- Knowing how the brain and the nervous system interpret information and influence symptoms in the body helps us work with a child's behaviors and impulses that we might traditionally judge as "bad."
- We're not consciously aware of the vast majority of information we take in.
- Trauma is entirely dependent on the perception of the event and whether we are able to integrate the sensory data.
- Our brains are primed to pause when they perceive an unknown.
- Incongruencies in the environment are registered as a threat in the brain.
- "*Shoulds*" are a challenge because they're perceived as a threat to our sense of self.

- When we "should" ourselves, we directly challenge our authentic self. We deny who we are and don't see our own wisdom. This can create an internal dilemma and activate the autonomic nervous system, which tries to handle the discrepancy.

- The autonomic nervous system has two sides: a sympathetic branch for revving us up and a parasympathetic branch for slowing us down. The sympathetic branch is responsible for the fight-or-flight response, and the parasympathetic branch is responsible for the freeze-or-fall asleep response, also referred to as the freeze-or-faint response.

- Our perception of the challenge or threat activates our nervous system into a hyper- or hypo-aroused response.

- If we perceive that we can do something about the challenge, our sympathetic branch will have an excessive response and the fight-or-flight system will be activated. Symptoms of the sympathetic branch include defensiveness, aggression, anxiety and overwhelm.

- Kids who are hypo-aroused often feel helpless and depressed and don't want to be seen. They seem tired, with not much affect or expression. At extreme levels, they're almost ghost-like and robotic.

- Therapists who perceive threats as they deal with the

intense aggression and death energy in the playroom for an extended period of time without regulating will probably begin to manifest signs of hypo-arousal.

- Children who are expressing excessive hyper-aroused symptoms (acting out) tend to be referred to therapy, but we need to make sure we aren't forgetting about the hypo-aroused children's need for support. Children in a hypo-aroused state perceive challenges as being too big, and they've already begun to shut down their emotional worlds. Children who are acting out still believe they have a chance.

- Every symptom and diagnosis a child brings into therapy is the result of a dys-regulated nervous system, which means an excessive activation of the sympathetic (hyper-aroused) or parasympathetic (hypo-aroused) branches.

- Aggression and death play are the symbolic forms of hyper-aroused and hypo-aroused states of the nervous system.

- When children or the play become aggressive and intense, their nervous systems are moving into a highly activated sympathetic response. When death shows up in the playroom, the room is filled with the energy of a highly activated parasympathetic response. These two energies often show up in pairs.

- When we understand that aggression and death are the

symbolic forms of the extreme arousal states of a child's nervous system, we can embrace a paradigm for healing based on nervous system regulation: All behavior, including aggression, is an attempt at regulation.

• When we help children move toward their intense emotional states and sensations, we're developing resiliency in the children while helping to re-pattern their nervous systems.

(Endnotes)

1   Schore,A.N. *Affect Regulation and the Repair of the Self* (NewYork:W.W.Norton, 2003), 37.

2   Dispenza, J. *Evolve Your Brain: The Science of Changing Your Mind* (Deerfield Beach: Health Communications, Inc., 2007).

3   Dispenza, J. *Evolve Your Brain:The Science of Changing Your Mind.*

CHAPTER 3

What Regulation Really Means

The more therapists I teach, the more aware I become that the concept of regulation or becoming regulated is often misunderstood. Many people think that being regulated means being calm, but that isn't always the case. From a Synergetic Play Therapy perspective, *regulated* means I'm mindful and aware of myself. In a moment of regulation, I can think clearly, I can make a conscious choice, I'm able to notice my breath, I'm able to feel grounded, I can speak clearly and I have an experience of being *in my body*. I'm connected to myself.

(Refer to the nervous system chart in Chapter 2.)

Regulation in the nervous system occurs when we become consciously aware of ourselves. In those moments, we're aware that we're separate from whatever is happening. We know that we're not the anger or the sadness. We're larger than that experience, if only for a brief moment. That moment of awareness empowers us to attach and connect to ourselves. We can therefore be regulated in our anger. We can be regulated in our sadness. We can be regulated in our anxiety.

As an example, let's say something totally irritates me. My perception of the challenge causes me to become dys-regulated and detach from myself. I end up in a state of hyper-arousal, and I'm not at all connected to myself. I'm feeling consumed by the sensation of irritation inside me. Then I become aware. I notice that I'm talking faster. I notice I'm tapping my fingers, my right leg is moving and my heart rate is picking up. I notice that my body feels activated inside. As the activation intensifies, I get a little dizzy. I start to notice and pay attention to everything I feel and see. As I do, I begin to come back to myself. I'm no longer detached. I can feel the intensity coursing through my body and I'm aware. I'm having moments of regulation during intensity and I definitely don't feel calm. This is the type of regulation we're trying to teach our child clients. We want them to learn how to reattach to them selves when they become dys-regulated so that they can manage the intensity that occurs inside them.

REGULATION EXISTS ON A CONTINUUM

You may have a brief moment of regulation or you may have many moments of regulation that add up to a state of regulation, in which you may feel calm. In the example I just gave, I was having moments of regulation. I mention this because it's important that as play therapists we understand that becoming calm is neither the goal nor the point of learning how to facilitate aggressive play in the playroom. The point is to learn how to manage the energy of our dys-regulated states and to teach children how to do the same. Understanding this is key to doing this work. If your goal is to stop the energy because you want the energy to calm down, you will inadvertently shut the child's process down or contain the child in a way that may encourage the energy to remain stuck or spinning within the child rather than being integrated.

We regulate to move toward the intensity, not to get out of it. Rather than stopping the energy in the playroom, let's teach our clients how to regulate through the intensity by teaching them to become mindful of their experience. This allows them to move toward their experience instead of running away from it, which can escalate the symptoms. It's through self-awareness that the energy in the aggressive and death play will begin to integrate and over time the child will naturally arrive at a state of regulation.

It's not practical to think a child will never be angry again, never want to hit a friend again or never talk back to an adult again. There will probably also be times when they want to run and hide and put their head under the covers and never come out again. What *is* practical and possible is teaching kids how to stay connected to themselves when they're faced with challenges. This is what facilitating aggressive and death play is all about. We want to help children stay connected to themselves during the intensity of their hyper- and hypo-aroused states so that they can integrate the energy and become self-aware. We want to teach them that they can feel it and notice it without being consumed by it.

THE BASICS OF REGULATING

Imagine that you're about to go swimming and the water is a bit cold. I go to the shores of Connecticut every summer, and even as I write this, I can feel the hairs on my arms stand up as I imagine the sensation of the cold water!

Now, I realize that you might be inclined to jump or dive into the water, but for this analogy, imagine that today you're feeling timid and your brain perceives the cold water as a challenge. You take a few steps into the water and immediately feel the cold water on your feet and ankles and it's a little shocking! So you stop and breathe through the sensations, and as your body adjusts, you take another step out and the water is now up to your knees.

If you're anything like me, your shoulders are up to your ears and you're opening and closing your hands attempting to manage the sensations and probably saying, "Cold, cold, cold," or something less G-rated. After a few minutes, you adjust and take another step. The water is now up to your belly. This one is hard. The sensation is a little more intense and you're tightening every muscle in your body, trying to handle the impact of the sensations. Again you breathe and try to help your body relax and adjust. Eventually, the temperature becomes tolerable and even refreshing. So it goes until eventually you're are actually swimming.

Now, let's look at what you automatically did to regulate as you moved into the cold water. First, you used *mindfulness* and *awareness* to develop a relationship with the sensations in your body. You also used *breathing* and *movement* to adjust to the intensity. You might even have yelled, shrieked or *named your experience out loud*: "Ah! This is freezing!" These are all strategies you automatically used to regulate through the intensity and move farther out into the water until you were completely "in it."

These are the exact same processes that can be used in the playroom. In Synergetic Play Therapy, we must regulate to keep our bodies from experiencing high states of dys-regulation, which can lead to burnout and symptoms of compassion fatigue. Remember, we use regulation to move toward the uncomfortable feelings and sensations instead of moving away from them. The moment we become aware of our experience, we are in relationship with the uncomfortable sensations and feelings and we can begin to regulate through them. It's worth repeating that the point of regulation is not to stop or avoid the experience—the point is to allow ourselves to move into the experience more deeply and with a greater level of mindfulness and awareness. In fact, learning how to move toward the challenging feelings and sensations is one of the most important parts of being able to remain present and hold the intensity in the playroom in such a way that the child can begin to integrate the energy.

MOVE TOWARD THE FEAR

Moving toward the intensity, remaining present and regulating through emotions and body sensations is an art—the art of being able to work with aggression and death in the playroom.

I've seen dozens of therapists develop signs of a dys-regulated nervous system and want to avoid the playroom or working with certain clients because their brains were screaming, "I'm scared and overwhelmed!" As a result, they backed away and avoided because they didn't know how to regulate and emotionally come back to the child (and themselves). By using the model I'm sharing, you can work with intense energy in the playroom. Not only will it help change the lives of your clients, but it will also help you become more authentic and resilient in your own life.

PUT *YOUR* OXYGEN MASK ON FIRST!

As children play and their nervous systems become activated, their memories, emotions and body sensations will begin to emerge. We'll feel the dys-regulated states of their nervous systems through a process called resonance, whether we're consciously aware or it or not. As we allow our sensations and emotions to come into conscious awareness, we increase our capacity to accurately attune to the client. What's so crucial about this is that in order for us to attune to our clients, we must first attune to ourselves.

When we fly on an airplane, before we take off the flight attendant gets on the speaker and announces the safety procedures to be followed in case of an emergency. One of the procedures we will hear is, "In case of loss of oxygen, an oxygen mask will fall from the compartment above you. If you're flying with a child or someone who needs help, please put your mask on *before* you assist them with theirs." Even airlines understand this principle. You have to help yourself breathe before you can help someone else! This principle is one of the foundations of learning how to teach regulation to your child clients. *You have to regulate yourself before you can help a child regulate.*

Here's the bottom line: You're going to become dys-regulated to some degree during intense play therapy sessions. Your brain is designed to perceive threats and challenges, as we've already discovered. The work is not to avoid and attempt to prevent this from happening but rather to learn how to regulate through it so you can teach your child client how to do it. In the process, you reinforce your own regulation ability as you model to the child options about how they might be able to manage theirs.

FEEL IT!

To attune to our clients, we must be open to our own bodily and emotional states.[1] [2] This means we need to stop trying to figure everything out in the playroom and begin to feel what's happening. I tell my students to get out of their heads and get into their bodies. Through your body you will be able to access all the information necessary to facilitate what's needed in that moment. Think of it this way: When a baby is screaming, an attuned caregiver doesn't stop and analyze the situation and try to figure out the best intervention for calming the baby—they instinctually pick up the baby and begin to rock, sway, make sounds, bounce and follow their instincts about what to do next. There's no map, just moment-to-moment attunement that reveals what to do. For caregivers to do this effectively, they're feeling their way through each moment. Facilitating aggression and death play is very similar.

When a therapist is emotionally attuned to the client, genuine emotional responses will be evoked in the therapist. "Much like the mother who is implicitly modeling for the child her own struggles to regulate her dys-regulated state, therapists must be able to resonate empathically with our clients, psychobiologically feeling their difficult, intense states. Without this ability to self-manage, we can't help the client to regulate. Such work implies a profound commitment by both participants in the therapeutic scenario and a deep emotional involvement on the therapist's part." [3] *Feel your way through the play—don't think your way through the play.*

In the next chapter, you'll learn a very important process involving projection and the mirror neuron system that occurs in play therapy, which in Synergetic Play Therapy we call "The Setup".

CHAPTER 3 KEY POINTS

- Regulation in the nervous system occurs when we become consciously aware of ourselves. We're aware that we're separate from whatever is happening. We're larger than that experience, if only for a brief moment.

- We want the children we work with to learn how to re-attach to themselves when they become dys-regulated so that they can manage the intensity that occurs inside them.

- Becoming calm is neither the goal nor the point of learning how to facilitate aggressive play in the playroom. If our goal is to stop the energy, we'll inadvertently shut the child's process down or contain the child in a way that may encourage the energy to remain stuck or spinning within the child rather than being integrated.

- We regulate to move toward the intensity, not to get out of it.

- Through self-awareness, the energy in the aggression and death play will begin to integrate and over time the child will naturally arrive at a state of regulation.

- When we're facilitating aggression and death play, we help children stay connected to themselves during the intensity of their hyper- and hypo-aroused states so they can integrate the energy and become self-aware. We want to teach them that they can feel it and notice it without being consumed by it.

- In Synergetic Play Therapy, we must regulate to keep our bodies from experiencing high states of dys-regulation, which can lead to burnout and symptoms of compassion fatigue.

- The point of regulation is to allow ourselves to move into an experience more deeply and with a greater level of mindfulness and awareness. Learning how to move toward the challenging feelings and sensations is one of the most important parts of being able to remain present and hold the intensity in the playroom so the child can begin to integrate the energy.

- We feel the dys-regulated states of a client's nervous system through a process called resonance, whether we're consciously aware or it or not. As we allow our sensations and emotions to come into conscious awareness, we increase our capacity to accurately attune to the client. In order for us to attune to a client, we must first attune to ourselves.

- We're going to become dys-regulated to some degree during intense play therapy sessions.

- We need to stop trying to figure everything out in the playroom and begin to feel what's happening. Through your body you will be able to access all the information necessary to facilitate what's needed in that moment.

(Endnotes)

1 Schore, A.N. *Affect Regulation and the Origin of the Self: The Neurobiology of Emotional Development* (New York: Erlbaum, 1994).

2 Siegel, D.J. *The Mindful Brain: Reflection and Attunement in the Cultivation of Well-Being* (New York: W.W. Norton, 2007).

3 Dales, S., and P. Jery. Attachment, affect regulation and mutual synchrony in adult psychotherapy. *American Journal of Psychotherapy* 2008; 62(3), 300.

CHAPTER 4

The Setup

"You have to sit here," my five-year-old client Mikey says as he points to a small pretend circle in the middle of the room. "It's an island, and you have to sit in it and you can't move away." These are the only words Mikey says to me. The rest of the session he's completely silent. As I sit there on my small island, my stomach starts to knot up. Realizing that if I move I will fall into the ocean, I feel anxiety begin to swirl inside me. I notice that I'm having a hard time taking a full breath. As this anxiety wells up inside me, a shark puppet starts circling my island, staring at me and taunting me.

I'm scared! I don't feel safe!

My breathing becomes shallow. My body is tense. The shark jumps out of the water and lunges at me. It grabs hold of my arm with its teeth and I scream. It won't let go! I have a shark biting my arm and it won't let go! *"It won't let go! It won't stop!"* I scream.

Finally, Mikey opens the shark's mouth, releasing my arm, and the shark goes back into the water and resumes circling my island. Feeling helpless, I try to catch my breath. Then, once again the shark jumps out of the water and bites me. It holds on tight with its teeth for what feels like minutes while I scream in pain.

Finally, Mikey again releases the shark's mouth and I sit there terrified, praying that it doesn't happen again.

FEELING WHAT THEY FEEL

> *"Remember always that whatsoever is happening around you is rooted in the mind. Mind is always the cause. It is the projector, and outside there are only screens—you project yourself." Osho*[1]

When kids come into our playroom, they set us up to feel how they feel. They also do this with the toys. This is truly the heart of the projective process in play therapy. As children set us up to feel how they feel, they have the opportunity to watch us manage the sensations and emotions we're holding. This understanding is often overlooked and misunderstood, yet it's one of the fundamental components of being able to understand what the child is trying to communicate.

The child projects his inner world onto the toys and therapist setting them up to experience his perception of what it feels like to be him. – Synergetic Play Therapy tenet

If a child feels anxious, you and the toys will be set up to feel anxious. If a child is struggling with rejection and not feeling good enough, you and the toys will be set up to feel rejected and not good enough. If a child is feeling overwhelmed, you and the toys will be set up to feel overwhelmed. If a child is feeling controlled, you'll be set up to feel controlled.

Reflection:

Take a moment and think about your last play therapy session. Put yourself back into the room with the child and let yourself feel what it was like to be in relationship with the child. Ask yourself, "What was I set up to feel? What were the toys set up to feel?" Consider what was happening with your nervous system. Were you hyper-aroused? Were you hypo-aroused? Did you flip-flop back and forth? Contemplate how this information is relevant to the child's world.

Let's go back to Mikey. What was I set up to feel? As I sat there, I was set up to feel anxious, trapped, terrified, in pain, unable to protect myself in any way, helpless and breathless. Shortly after Mikey was born, his parents realized he had a lot of tactile sensitivities. He also struggled with breathing and had frequent panic attacks as a young child. Often, these panic attacks would require hospitalization, during which he'd be held down to receive injections and have monitors placed on his body. Let's imagine what Mikey's perception of these experiences might have been. Might he have felt anxious? Terrified? In pain from the injections and the feeling of monitors on his sensitive skin? Unable to move away or protect himself? Helpless? Having a hard time breathing? Although we can't know for sure, we can speculate that this might have been his experience.

Mikey did whatever he needed to do to "set me up" to experience his perception of himself and things that have happened to him, and then he watched how I handled it. He was also spending a lot of time in his life "setting others up" to feel what was going on inside him in his attempt to integrate these feelings and sensations. The primary reason he was brought in for therapy was that he was aggressive, often scaring people in a shocking way and attempting to physically hurt them. From the perspective of the "setup," we can see that Mikey was doing everything he could to show everyone around him what he was experiencing inside.

Unfortunately, everyone was shutting him down and telling him he had to stop instead of teaching and modeling to him how to handle the intensity that was arising in his hyperaroused nervous system. They didn't understand that his aggression was an attempt at communication and regulation. It's important to note that knowing Mikey's history wasn't necessary for me to work with him this way. To do this work, we don't need to know the backstory. You will still be set up, and with what you're learning you'll be able to help your clients integrate the challenging memories and the corresponding sensations and feelings they carry inside.

CHILDREN ARE NATURAL REGULATORS

All behavior is an attempt at regulation (connecting back to self), even the behaviors that society might label "inappropriate." Children bite, hit, yell, push, throw tantrums, hide, avoid making eye contact and refuse to talk in an attempt to regulate by bringing in or shutting out sensory data. Children also wiggle, sing, roll around on the floor, jump, push against things, hang upside down, play, create art and engage in many other actions to regulate. They're brilliant and will do whatever is necessary to manage the emotions and sensations that are arising in their bodies.

The challenge occurs when a child's strategies for regulation aren't effective, keeping him in a state of dys-regulation, and when his regulation strategy is negatively affecting his life. The more time a child spends in the fight/flight/freeze/fall asleep response, the higher the probability that the child will experience problems in areas such as health, relationship, learning, rage and depression, and impulsivity.

Although children have a natural instinct to regulate, they need help with learning how to regulate effectively. They seek out help by watching how others manage their emotions and bodily sensations.

MODELING REGULATION

According to Daniel Siegel, when a client's painful memories and emotional states are reactivated and are outside the client's window of tolerance (the capacity to integrate sensory data), the client will begin to move away from those emotions in an attempt to avoid the intensity.[2] The act of moving away from the experience reinforces the message in the brain that there is a threat or a challenge and keeps the nervous system in a state of dys-regulation.

The same is true for us. If we aren't willing to be authentic and experience our own bodily, emotional and cognitive states while working toward modulating these inner experiences, we'll move away from these states[3], potentially leaving our client feeling unsafe and unseen.[4]

Allan Schore explains that as challenging emotional states or enactments enter the play precipitated by the child client, the attuned therapist uses mindfulness to attempt to open to these internal feelings and sensations and not move away or defend against them[5]. The therapist is then able to begin to modulate the intensity using authentic dialogue describing cognitive, emotional and sensorimotor states, along with modeling regulation of bodily sensations through breath and movement.[6]

Bonnie Badenoch, PhD, author of *The Brain Wise Therapist*, says:

> When the relationship is experienced as safe enough, the dissociated experiences will begin to come into conscious awareness. As we resonate together, the activation will amplify and, if our window of tolerance is broad enough

to contain this energy and information, our patient will also experience a widening of his or her window. In the research of Carl Marci and colleagues,[7] these moments of autonomic synchrony were subjectively experienced as empathetically rich interpersonal joining. This research showed that within the session, our nervous systems will flow into, out of, and back into synchrony many times. This rhythm is parallel to the dance of mother and infant as they move from attunement to rupture and back to repair over and over, laying the foundation for security, optimism, and resilience.[8]

The syncratic dance beautifully describes the interaction Mikey and I had as he began to learn from my modeling that it was okay to go toward his fear and not run away from it. He didn't learn how to manage his hyper-arousal in one session, of course, but over the next few sessions he was able to move toward regulating his own nervous system.

REGULATION TECHNIQUES

Let's go back to the scenario of me attempting to wade into the cold Connecticut water in Chapter 3. As the sensation of the water entered my *awareness,* I had to use *mindfulness,* and *breath, movement* and *naming my experience out loud* as ways to allow me to move toward the challenging sensations.

Now let's explore how these techniques were used with Mikey and the effect it had on both Mikey and me.

Mindfulness

> *"Mindfulness means being awake. It means knowing what you are doing." — Jon Kabat-Zinn, Wherever You Go, There You Are: Mindfulness Meditation in Everyday Life* [9]

We're all familiar with the idea that you can't change something unless you become aware that you're doing it. The same is true in the playroom. Children aren't always aware of what they're doing in the therapy session (remember that we're consciously aware of less than 1 percent of all the data we receive). For us to become aware of what we're doing requires mindfulness. Mindfulness is the act of becoming aware of what is.

This important aspect of growth is why we spend so much time as therapists engaging in reflective listening and mirroring back to our clients what we hear them say. It's also why we track the child's play using observation statements. As therapists, we're attempting to help our clients engage in mindfulness, becoming aware of what they are saying, doing and feeling.

As Mikey was setting me up to feel his perception of himself and his world, it was crucial that I use mindfulness to become aware of what I was feeling and experiencing. Had I not been aware of the intensity of the energy in my body, the challenge to breathe, the feelings of fear inside me and the overall experience of not feeling safe, I wouldn't have been able to effectively modulate the dys-regulation and activation in my nervous system. As a result, I wouldn't have been able to model to Mikey how to regulate through the intensity. Through the act of mindfulness, becoming aware of what I was experiencing, I would have missed the information I needed to understand what Mikey was setting me up to feel and missed the information I needed to understand what I needed to do to take care of myself while modeling regulation for him.

Breath

> *"Regulate the breathing, and thereby control the mind."* — B.K.S. Iyengar[10]

The way we breathe dramatically affects our nervous system. In fact, when we become dys-regulated, so does our breathing and vice versa. Did you know you can create a state of dys-regulation in your body simply by breathing a certain way? When you're breathing in a shallow way (when your inhalation is longer than your exhalation), you can activate your sympathetic nervous system, creating feelings of anxiety and overwhelm. When your exhalation is longer than your inhalation for an extended period of time, you'll begin to feel the symptoms of hypo-arousal as your parasympathetic nervous system becomes activated. When we're in the midst of intense aggression and death play, our breathing becomes affected as our autonomic nervous system becomes activated. One of the best ways to regulate and manage the intensity we're experiencing in the playroom is through our breath.

When I first sat down on the island that Mikey created for me, I noticed that my breathing changed. I could feel a tightening in my chest as it became harder to take a full breath. When I noticed this, I took a deep breath to allow for more air to enter my lungs. Once the shark entered the play and began to circle me, the perception that I wasn't safe influenced my breathing, creating the sensation of little space in my lungs as I simultaneously felt the quickening of my heart rate. My breathing became more shallow. When the shark bit my arm and wouldn't let go, I noticed a feeling of panic entering my body and I consciously worked toward elongating my exhale to counter the contraction. When the shark let go and returned to the water, I began to regulate myself by taking full breaths, allowing my body to discharge the energy that had just built up in the play. I used my breath to modulate the intensity of the sympathetic response I was experiencing in order to keep me present and attuned with Mikey.

Movement

"The body always leads us home . . . if we can simply learn to trust sensation and stay with it long enough for it to reveal appropriate action, movement, insight, or feeling."[11] — *Pat Ogden*

When the goal is to teach children how to regulate through challenging emotions and sensations, it's essential for movement to be part of the therapeutic process. Without movement, the child will have a difficult time learning how to navigate the landscape in which the challenging energy arises. As play therapists, we use movement for three reasons:

- Movement helps us become aware of what we're experiencing.
- Movement is a way to regulate our nervous systems and not get stuck in a dys-regulated state.
- Our movement gives the child permission to also use movement as a way to manage his or her internal states.

Even though I was told I had to stay on my small island and my lower body couldn't move, I could move my upper body and arms. In between the shark bites when the shark was circling the island, I took advantage of the pause in intensity to allow my upper body to move and release some of the buildup. I tended to my wound by holding my arm and rubbing around the bite, modeling self-care and connection. I also rubbed and squeezed my legs to create energy flow so that the trauma energy wouldn't get stuck in the lower half of my body. And I rubbed my hand over my heart and gently rocked back and forth as a way to ground and connect with myself. The entire time I did this, Mikey watched me.

There wasn't a right way to move—I simply trusted what my body needed and followed the information, keeping in mind that whatever I chose to do needed to be within the context of the play that I was set up to experience. For example, I did not stand up and shake it out, since the point was for me to stay in a small area, feeling trapped and anxious. I modeled regulation within the energy of the setup.

NAME YOUR EXPERIENCE OUT LOUD

Of all the ways to regulate, naming your experience out loud seems to be the scariest for most play therapists. Many play therapists believe that it's not okay to name your experience out loud for fear of overwhelming the child or setting the child up to take care of the therapist. I find this interesting considering that we spend a lot of time teaching parents to do this. We teach parents about the importance of naming their emotions out loud, yet we don't do it in the playroom. In the context of parenting, we honor and encourage adults to name their experiences with an understanding that when they do so, they are modeling and teaching their children about the world of emotions.

According to Daniel Siegel and Tina Bryson, naming internal experiences out loud allows a person to move through painful states and helps regulate the nervous system.[12] Siegel coined the term "Name it to tame it" to describe the calming effect that naming your experience out loud has on the amygdala in the brain.[13] [14] Naming your experience out loud allows you to remain present with what is in your conscious awareness and move toward greater flexibility in your internal states. At the same time, according to Allan Shore, blood flows to the right prefrontal cortex of the brain, a process essential to emotional regulation.[15]

As I was playing with Mikey, I allowed myself to describe my internal experiences out loud. I said things like "I'm scared!" and "I don't feel safe!" when the shark was circling my island. When I first sat down on my island, I said, "I'm noticing that my tummy is in a knot and I feel anxious," and, "I'm having a

hard time taking a deep breath." During and after the shark attacks, I authentically cried out in pain. I used naming my experience out loud as a way to regulate myself and to make Mikey
aware of several factors that would encourage him to regulate.
First, verbalizing the experience told Mikey I understood what
it felt like to be him. It also gave him the language to describe
the various emotional states and physical sensations I was being
set up to feel. And it gave him permission to name his experiences when he needs to.

Consciously feeling the intensity and moving toward the
heightened emotional state models to the child that it's okay to
move toward the experience instead of running away from it.[16][17][18]

As Mikey began to intensify the play, I had to connect to myself and be willing to feel and move toward the uncomfortable
sensations arising in my body so that I could act as an external
regulator helping to modulate the intensity in the room. By staying open to my body sensations and emotions, I was also able to
remain present and attuned to him. As Siegel explains it, when a
therapist is willing to feel what a client is feeling, the client feels
felt by the therapist.[19] It was the feeling of being felt by me that
allowed Mikey to feel safe enough to move toward the memories, feelings, and sensations he was struggling to integrate.

Within sessions, Mikey's breathing patterns and sensitivity

to touch changed. His parents reported that he was able to talk about how he was feeling in ways he hadn't been able to do before and that his aggressive behavior diminished significantly. Through the process, my own nervous system's capacity expanded and I learned how to adapt to a new type of intensity. By using regulation, I was able to modulate the dys-regulation in my nervous system, keeping me grounded and connected to myself. As the intensity emerged, I was able to feel it, move it and let it go. As Mikey observed this process, he learned to do the same.

In the next chapter, I'll explain why it's so important for us to be authentic in our responses rather than to merely role-play.

CHAPTER 4 KEY POINTS

- When kids come into our playroom, they set us up to feel how they feel. This is a critical component of how a play therapist and child communicate.

- We don't need to know a child's history to effectively work with him or her. The "setup" alone gives us what we need to help the child.

- All behavior is an attempt at regulation (connecting back to self), even the behaviors that society might label "inappropriate."

- The more time a child spends in the fight/flight/freeze/fall asleep response, the higher the probability that the child will experience problems in areas such as health, relationship, learning, rage and depression cycles, and impulsivity.

- Although children have a natural instinct to regulate, they need help learning how to regulate effectively. They seek out help by watching how others manage their emotions and bodily sensations.

- Through the projective process, we give children an opportunity to observe their own feelings in action. By watching us, they're learning how to better regulate. We teach children how to better regulate through modeling

- We can openly regulate our nervous system in challenging emotional and sensory states through mindfulness, breath, movement and naming the experience out loud.[20] Regulating while moving toward an intense emotional or sensory state models to children a way they can connect to themselves.

- Moving away from an experience reinforces the message in the brain that there's a threat or a challenge, which keeps the nervous system in a state of dys-regulation.

- If we aren't willing to be authentic and experience our own bodily, emotional and cognitive states while working toward modulating these inner experiences, we'll move away from these states, potentially leaving our client feeling unsafe and unseen.

- When the goal is to teach children how to regulate through challenging emotions and sensations, it's essential for movement to be part of the therapeutic process. Without movement, the child will have a difficult time learning how to navigate the landscape in which the challenging energy arises.

- As therapists, we attempt to help our clients engage in mindfulness, becoming aware of what they are saying, doing and feeling.

- The way we breathe dramatically affects our nervous system. When we become dys-regulated, so does our breathing and vice versa. One of the best ways to regulate and manage the intensity we're experiencing in the playroom is through our breath.

- Naming your experience out loud allows you to stay present with what's in your conscious awareness and move toward greater flexibility in your internal states.

- Consciously feeling the intensity and moving toward the heightened emotional state models to the child that it's okay to move toward the experience instead of running away from it.

(Endnotes)

1   Osho, *The Book of Nothing: Hsin Hsin Ming*, Talk #5

2   Siegel, D.J. *The Mindful Therapist: A Clinician's Guide to Mindsight and Neural Integration.* (New York: W.W. Norton, 2010).

3   Schore, A. N. *Affect Regulation and the Origin of the Self: The Neurobiology of Emotional Development* (New York: Erlbaum, 1994).

4   Siegel, *The Mindful Therapist: A Clinician's Guide to Mindsight and Neural Integration.*

5   Schore, A.N. *The Science of the Art of Psychotherapy.* (New York: W.W. Norton, 2011).

6   Ogden, P., K. Minton and C. Pain. *Trauma and the Body: A Sensorimotor Approach to Psychotherapy.* (New York: W.W. Norton, 2006).

7   Marci, C.D., and Reiss, H. The clinical relevance of psychophysiology: Support for the psychobiology of empathy and psychodynamic process. *American Journal of Psychotherapy* 2005: 259, 213-226.

8   Badenoch, B. *The Brain Savvy Therapist's Workbook.* (New York: W.W. Norton, 2011).

9   Kabat-Zinn, J. *Wherever You Go, There You Are: Mindfulness Meditation in Everyday Life.* (New York: Hyperion, 1995).

10 Iyengar, B.K.S. *Light on Yoga: Yoga Dipika.* (New York: Schocken Books, 1979).

11 Ogden et al., *Trauma and the Body: A Sensorimotor Approach to Psychotherapy*.

12 Siegel, D.J., and T.P. Bryson. *The Whole Brain Child: Revolutionary Strategies to Nurture Your Child's Developing Mind*. New York: Delacorte Press, 2011).

13 Siegel, *The mindful Therapist: A Clinician's Guide to Mindsight and Neural Integration*.

14 Siegel, D.J., and T.P. Bryson. *The Whole Brain Child: Revolutionary Strategies to Nurture Your Child's Developing Mind*.

15 Schore, *Affect Regulation and the Origin of the Self: The Neurobiology of Emotional Development*.

16 Siegel, *The mindful Therapist: A Clinician's Guide to Mindsight and Neural Integration*.

17 Ogden et al., *Trauma and the Body: A Sensorimotor Approach to Psychotherapy*.

18 Ogden, P., C. Pain, K. Minton and J. Fisher. Including the body in mainstream psychotherapy for traumatized individuals. *Psychologist-Psychoanalyst* 2005; 25(4), 19-24.

19 Siegel, *The Mindful Brain: Reflection and Attunement in the Cultivation of Well-Being*.

20 Ogden et al., *Trauma and the Body: A Sensorimotor Approach to Psychotherapy*.

CHAPTER 5

Authentic Expression

"There's a ghost behind you!" Jack shouted.

"I'm scared! I'm scared!" I said, putting my right hand on my heart and the other hand on my stomach. I exhaled loudly in an attempt to ground myself.

"And one over there, and another one there," he said, pointing to the corner of the room. "They're gonna hurt you!"

"I'm so scared. I don't feel safe. I don't have any protection," I said while continuing to breathe and hold on to myself.

Jack rolled his blue eyes. "Whatever. We're just playing."

At five years old, Jack had already learned how to emotionally shut down and he was trying to shut down my emotional expression, too. Jack came to me because his parents were concerned about his high levels of aggression and what they referred to as his "irrational fears." During the intake with his mother, it was obvious that she was frustrated with him and emotionally disconnected from herself. When I asked her how she felt about his anger and fears, she looked at me and bluntly said, "I don't do anger." She then went on to share that his obsession with ghosts was just too much for her.

In our first play session together, Jack set me up to feel an overwhelming sense of fear along with a clear message that it wasn't okay for me to express my feelings. After Jack introduced the ghosts to the play, he told me there were bad guys in the hallway that might enter the room at any second.

I allowed myself to feel and express an authentic response based on how I would actually feel if there were ghosts in the room and bad guys in the hallway. I also allowed myself to regulate throughout the hyper-arousal, because the hyper-vigilance was intense! Each time I expressed my fear, I noticed that I was placing one hand on my heart and the other on my stomach. I didn't plan to do that. It was my body's natural response. Each time I expressed fear, Jack made fun of me and tried to shut me down even though he was trying to scare me. He'd mock me, saying things like "I'm never scared. I'm not scared of anything." Yet he placed every toy gun, sword, shield, grenade and even a pair of handcuffs in front of the door just in case the bad guys got in.

Two sessions later, Jack and I were playing in the sand tray and I saw him hide a plastic snake under the sand behind a boy figurine, and once again I felt the fear rise up inside me and once again I allowed myself to have an authentic reaction. "There's that feeling inside me again," I whispered hesitantly. "I feel scared, but I'm worried I can't say it because I might get told I'm not allowed to be scared."

Jack looked at me and stood up straight. "I get scared," he announced. This was the first time he'd acknowledged his fear and not made fun of me.

I felt my body relax and I could feel the significance of the moment. I took a deep breath to hold the space for him. "You do?"

"Yes. I even know what to do when I get scared."

"What do you do?" I asked, breathing deeply to hold this poignant moment.

"Watch," he said as he put one hand on his heart and the other on his stomach and let out a long breath.

I'd never told Jack to stop and take a deep breath when he was scared. He saw me do it and learned by watching me. My willingness to show my fear and move toward it allowed him to learn a coping strategy to regulate his nervous system. I was being authentic, and it gave Jack the space to be authentic, too. He knew I was being *real* and was in tune with him, so he felt more comfortable being real with me. By working with Jack in this way, I was helping him to change synaptic connections by engaging his mirror neuron system. As he observed me modeling self-regulation in the midst of an intense emotion, he learned that he didn't have to deny his own emotions and sensations but rather could embrace them and learn how to regulate through them.

WE LEARN THROUGH OBSERVATION

It's well-understood that children learn how to regulate their own emotions by watching and perceiving their caregivers' responses. Children are able to learn through observation because of the mirror neuron system.[1][2] It's the "I feel what you feel" emotional empathy system. We can use it to get in sync with other people's emotions by reading facial expressions and body language and interpreting tone of voice.

When we observe an action over and over, this system makes it possible for us to understand the actions of others and imitate those actions.[3] It helps our minds to make a simulated mental model of what we observe and then imitate what we've seen.[4] To see a great example of how this works, watch what happens in a preschool class when one of the kids yawns. Like a chain reaction, most of the other kids will yawn. Another example of the mirror neuron system at work is when an infant attempts to stick out his tongue because he's watching Mommy or Daddy do it. Observing his parents automatically activates his mirror neurons that prime the motor neurons, activating the tongue to stick out.

This phenomenon helps explain why role-modeling is such a key component of the learning process. In the therapeutic process, it's speculated that the mirror neuron system makes it possible for the therapist and the client to share closely resonant interactions. The result is that through modeling, a child is able to watch his play therapist and learn how to regulate through challenging emotions that arise during their play, which is one of the primary goals with children who are engaging in aggression and death play.

CAN I REALLY BE ME?

When we talk about authenticity, we tend to think, "Well, of course we've got to be authentic with the child." But I've found there is some resistance to being ourselves in relationship with our child clients. I can't tell you how many times I've heard play therapists say, "I can't say that to a child," or, "I can't do that!" We get so worried about emotionally hurting children or putting them in a position where they might think they need to rescue us that we don't realize that the withholding of our authentic experience potentially leaves the child feeling "missed" and "not connected" to themselves and the therapist.

I assure you that it's okay to be yourself in the playroom. In fact, it's necessary if you're going to help a child regulate through intense play, because when we're not willing to be authentic, the child will usually amp up the play to get us to have an authentic response. I have never seen a child damaged because the therapist was "real." However, I have seen children who never deeply connected to their therapists and didn't go as deep as they could have gone because their therapists were too scared to share and express their authentic experience congruently. I have also seen children not be able to integrate the dys-regulated states of their nervous systems during aggressive and death play because their therapists didn't allow themselves to be authentic and model self-regulation.

It's important to distinguish between role-playing and allowing yourself to feel and express authentic emotions. Role-playing is a form of acting. When we're in a sword fight with a child, unless we allow ourselves to imagine that the swords are real and respond accordingly, we will be faking our responses and the child will know we're not being authentic. The more we can allow our minds to embrace what the setup would feel like if it were really happening, the more authentic our response will be and the more congruent it will be in the eyes of the child we are playing with.

"SHOULDS" GET IN THE WAY

In the upcoming chapters, I'll share some practical things to do in the playroom when the aggression and death play intensifies in a hyper-aroused or hypo-aroused direction. But before I do that, it's important that we take a moment to look at all the "shoulds" and "shouldn'ts" that prevent us from being truly authentic in the playroom. I realize that being completely authentic is a radical idea for many therapists, but I can tell you firsthand that it's highly effective and necessary.

Reflection:

> Write down all the shoulds and shouldn'ts that come to mind when you think about being authentic with a child. Common examples that I hear are "I shouldn't tell

a child that I'm angry," "I shouldn't tell a child what I'm feeling because they might want to take care of me" and "I shouldn't be completely authentic because it might be too much for the child." After you write your list, get curious about where you learned these messages.

SHARING OUR AUTHENTIC REACTIONS

In a Synergetic Play Therapy context, *authenticity* refers to being attuned to ourselves and the child so that we can have an authentic reaction *in response* to the child-initiated play. It doesn't mean sharing our personal lives or telling a child that when he handcuffed you and put you in jail, it reminded you of being punished with a "timeout" when you were his age. Authenticity in the playroom means being genuine and congruent about our internal states as they relate to the play that children initiate and the stories they share.

Essentially, kids are looking for two things in the intense play:

- Can the therapist hold the energy and hang in there?
- Is the therapist acting or being real?

If I'm having a robust sword fight with a child and I'm laughing or I have a big smile on my face, I'm probably not being authentic. If I'm having a sword fight and I look scared but I'm not willing to say it out loud and I pretend I'm fine, I'm also not being authentic. If I look anxious or shut down or show other signs of being dys-regulated but the words I'm saying are not congruent with my appearance, the child will pick up on my incongruence. In all these instances, I'm missing the opportunity to model how to regulate my nervous system in the midst of a challenge. I'm also giving the child a reason to increase the intensity of the play to try to get me to show up authentically, because most likely my lack of authenticity is registering as a threat to the child.

Since more than 60 percent of communication is nonverbal, we need to be mindful of our actions as much as our words. This is even more important with children, because they pay much more attention to what we're doing than what we're saying. They're not listening to our words as much as they're reading us and feeling us out by watching our body language and facial expressions. They're assessing us, taking in data and determining whether we're safe or we're a threat. If something about us doesn't make sense to them, their brains will potentially consider us a threat. At minimum, they will spend time trying to figure us out than allowing themselves to fully go into the play.

IT'S REAL TO THE CHILD, SO IT NEEDS TO BE REAL TO YOU

Sometimes therapists have a challenging time accessing the depth of their feelings or sensations, because they're being attacked by a pool noodle or a puppet, not a sword or something literally dangerous. Did you know that the brain can't tell the difference between something that is actually happening to you and something you're imagining? With this in mind, remember that children are trying to set you up to feel their perception of themselves and their world, which means that whatever is happening feels real to them. So it needs to feel real to you in order to access the authentic response they're looking for.

This is a very important point to understand. I tell my students to imagine that whatever is happening to them or whatever they're witnessing is real. I ask them to respond as if it were really happening. The moment they do, out comes an authentic response that's congruent with the energy in the room. The risk of not doing this is that children will continue to amp it up until you eventually have an authentic response that mirrors the feelings in their inner world or they give up.

Let's explore this a little deeper. You might be wondering, "But aren't I being authentic if I'm really not scared by a pool noodle or a puppet? Isn't expressing fear, when I know it's a puppet and isn't really going to hurt me, being *in*authentic?" And the answers are "yes" and "no." What I find with scenarios like this is that the therapist is focusing on the nonthreatening toy itself instead of feeling the energy that's arising because of the way the child is using the toy. The trick is to have both experiences so that you don't emotionally flood or get absorbed by the experience but are still able to be present in the intensity. You have to be in the experience, feeling the sensations and emotions that arise, while simultaneously having the awareness that you're not really in danger. You can do this with mindfulness and regulation. If you believe you really are in danger or you're about to leave your window of tolerance, it's time to set a boundary, as we'll discuss in the next chapter.

CHANGING THE NEURAL PATHWAYS

In Synergetic Play Therapy, the therapists try to be as authentic and congruent as possible during the play session. In doing so, we transmit the trust and safety our clients need for healing from the intensity of their traumatic experiences. The therapist's authenticity helps maximize attunement, allowing the therapist to serve as an external regulator for the client's dys-regulated states.[5] In other words, when we're being authentic, we can play a critical role in teaching kids how to regulate their nervous systems and change their brain activity. As Badenoch and Siegel explain, when the child's mirror neuron system is activated, the therapist's mindfulness and authentic expression can trigger new brain activity that can become associated with the feelings in the neural nets of memories.[6][7]

When children repeatedly see us being authentic and present in the midst of the activation of the dys-regulated states of the nervous system, their old programming can be interrupted, creating an opening for a new experience and giving them permission to move toward challenging internal states the way they see us do it. As children move toward their challenging internal states, new neural connections can be created and eventually initiate new neural organization.[8][9] We now know that with dedicated amounts of repetition, neural systems can change; however, we also know that most therapeutic interventions don't achieve that goal.[10]

When Jack brought the feeling of anxiety to life in the playroom, he simultaneously witnessed me repeatedly putting my hand on my chest and my stomach for self-care while taking a deep breath. Within only a few sessions he was able to move toward the intensity and eventually try the self-regulation behaviors modeled for him. It required a commitment from me to be authentic for this to occur.

I stayed as authentic as I could in the midst of his making fun of me, trying to shut me down and doing everything he could to scare me. I understood that everything occurring was part of the setup and that my job was to help him feel "felt" and to help him integrate the intensity while offering options for self-regulation through modeling. The result was that Jack was able to create new neural connections that resulted in a new neural organization. What's thrilling is that when we work with kids this way, every session has the potential to help them to integrate new information and rewire past encoded experiences.[11] [12] [13]

In the next chapter, you'll get some helpful insights about setting boundaries and some examples of how to set them without shutting down your client.

CHAPTER 5 KEY POINTS

- As children observe us modeling self-regulation in the midst of an intense emotion, they learn that they don't have to deny their own emotions and sensations but rather can embrace them and learn how to regulate through them.

- Children are able to learn through observation because of the mirror neuron system.[14] The mirror neuron system is the "I feel what you feel" emotional empathy system. Because of this system, we can get in sync with other people's emotions by reading facial expressions and body language and interpreting tone of voice.

- In the therapeutic process, it's speculated that the mirror neuron system makes it possible for the therapist and the client to share closely resonant interactions.

- The withholding of our authentic experience can potentially leave children feeling "missed" and "not connected" to themselves or to us, as their therapist.

- When we're not being authentic, the child will usually amp up the play to evoke an authentic response.

- The more we can allow our minds to embrace what the setup would feel like if it were really happening, the more authentic our response will be and the more congruent it will be in the eyes of the child we are playing with.

- Being completely authentic is a radical idea for many therapists, but it's necessary and highly effective.

- In a Synergetic Play Therapy context, *authenticity* refers to being attuned to ourselves and the child so that we can have an authentic reaction in response to the child-initiated play.

- Authenticity in the playroom means being genuine and congruent about our internal states as they relate to the play that children initiate and the stories they share.

- More than 60 percent of communication is nonverbal, so we need to be mindful of our actions as much as our words. This is even more important with children, because they pay much more attention to what we're doing than what we're saying.

- The brain can't tell the difference between something that is actually happening to you and something you're imagining.

- Since children are trying to set you up to feel their perception of themselves and their world, whatever is happening feels real to them and it needs to feel real to you in order to access the authentic response they're seeking.

- The risk of not authentically responding is that children will continue to amp it up until you have an authentic response that mirrors the feelings in their inner world or they'll give up.

- You have to be in the experience, feeling the sensations and emotions that arise, while simultaneously having the awareness that you're not really in danger. You can do this with mindfulness and regulation.

- By being as authentic and congruent as possible during the play session, we transmit the trust and safety our clients need for healing from the intensity of their traumatic experiences.

- When we're being authentic, we can play a critical role in teaching kids how to regulate their nervous systems and change their brain activity.

- When children repeatedly see us being authentic and present in the midst of the activation of the dys-regulated states of the nervous system, their old programming can be interrupted, creating an opening for a new experience and giving them permission to move toward challenging internal states the way they see us do it.

- As children move toward their challenging internal states, new neural connections can be created and eventually initiate new neural organization.

- With dedicated amounts of repetition, neural systems

can change, but most therapeutic interventions don't achieve that goal.

- Every play therapy session has the potential to help our clients to integrate new information and rewire their past encoded experiences.

(Endnotes)

1 Iacobini, M. *Face to Face: The Neural Basis for Social Mirroring and Empathy.* Psychiatric Annals, 2007.

2 Rizzolatti, g., Fogassi, L. & Gallese, V. Neurophysiological mechanisms underlying the understanding and imitation of action. *Nature Review Neuroscience, 2, 660-670.*

3 Bandura, A. *Social Learning Theory.* (NJ: Prentice Hall, 1977).

4 Heyes, C. Evolution, development and intentional control of imitiation. *Philosophical Transactions of the Royal Society B*, 364, 2293-2298.

5 Schore, A. N. *Affect Regulation and the Origin of the Self: The Neurobiology of Emotional Development* (New York: Erlbaum, 1994).

6 Badenoch, B.. *Being a Brain-Wise Therapist: A Practical Guide to Interpersonal Neurobiology.* (New York: W.W. Norton, 2008).

7 Siegel, D.J. *The Developing Mind: How Relationships and the Brain Interact to Shape Who We Are.* (New York: Guilford Press, 1999).

8 Edelman, G. M. *Neural Darwinism.* (New York: Basic Books, 1987).

9 Tyson, P. The challenges of psychoanalytic developmental theory. *Journal of the American Psychoanalytic Association* 2002; 50(1), 19-52.

10 Perry, B. D. Applying principles of neurodevelopment to clinical work with maltreated and traumatized children: The neurosequential model of therapeutics. In *Working with Traumatized Youth in Child Welfare*, Ed. N.B. Webb (New York: Guilford Press, 2006) 27-52.

11 Schore, *Affect Regulation and the Origin of the Self: The Neurobiology of Emotional Development.*

12 Siegel, *The Developing Mind: How Relationships and the Brain Interact to Shape Who We Are.*

13 Badenoch, *Being a Brain Wise Therapist: A Practical Guide to Interpersonal Neuro biology.*

14 Iacobini, M. *Face to Face: The Neural Basis for Social Mirroring and Empathy.*

CHAPTER 6

Setting Boundaries

Sarah, age six, walked over to the toy shelf and quickly spotted the handcuffs. She picked them up and closely examined the lock, as if attempting to discover whether they'd do the job. When she turned around and looked directly at her therapist, his eyes widened and his breathing changed. He was visibly anxious. She ran toward him, grabbed his arm and tried to force it behind his back, but he pulled his arm away from her. "We can't do that in here," he said. "It's not okay to handcuff me." Sarah was stunned. Her body language and facial expression spoke volumes. She thought she'd done something terribly wrong.

I saw this exchange during a play therapy session observation. I'm sharing this story to shed light on new possibilities. We've all set boundaries out of fear or frustration and then questioned whether the boundary was actually necessary or regretted the way we'd gone about it. Setting boundaries is an extremely important and somewhat controversial topic. There are many beliefs and ideas about how to do it, when to do it and even why a therapist needs to do it, but the vast majority of therapists I meet don't have a lot of clarity about when, how and why to set a limit.

We have to stop and ask ourselves this important question: What is the point of the boundary?

I've asked my students this question hundreds of times, and inevitably their responses are something like "I don't know. Isn't that what I'm supposed to do?" or "The child can't act like that in the session. I have to teach them appropriate ways to behave" or "It's not okay for me or my toys to be treated that way."

Before we explore a new way of understanding and working with boundaries, answer the following question.

Reflection:

Take a moment and think about why you set boundaries in the playroom? (It might help to think of a child you have set a boundary with and answer the question with that child in mind.) Take another moment to write your answers down.

Your answers are not right or wrong. What you've written is information about your beliefs and your window of tolerance. As you read this chapter, I encourage you to reflect on your answers. When you finish the chapter, read your written response and see if you'd like to revise or add to it in any way.

BOUNDARIES ARE PERSONAL!

What I'm about to introduce might conflict with other ideas you've heard about setting boundaries. If you find yourself shaking your head, furrowing your brow or pursing your lips, that's great! As play therapists, it's important for us to question our thinking and be open to shifting our paradigms regarding what "should" or "shouldn't" happen in a play therapy session.

Reflection:

Read what you wrote down. How much of it is based on a "should" or a belief about what is appropriate behavior?

Therapists can find themselves struggling with an internal conflict the moment they think a boundary might be necessary.

If a boundary is set because we think we're "supposed to" or "should" set one, we might not feel confident about our decision and question ourselves afterward. Remember that "shoulds" are felt as a threat to the self and get in the way of authenticity!

Sometimes a therapist sets a boundary because he or she truly believes the boundary is necessary to teach a child about appropriate behavior, but then feels a bit disconnected from the child or wonders why the child has pulled back, like in the story at the beginning of this chapter. I'm sharing these examples not to judge what was good or bad but because they have information that can help us.

When we become clear about why we're setting the boundary, we can do it in a way that doesn't cause the child or ourselves to feel shame.

BOUNDARIES ARE IMPORTANT!

When setting a boundary, it's important that you still get to be yourself and so does the child. We can achieve this if we shift our rationale for why we're setting the boundaries in the first place.

Are you ready for the new paradigm? Take a deep breath, move your body as you read this and regulate so that you can take this in.

Kids don't need boundaries in the playroom—therapists do!

Let's go back to Chapter 2 where we discussed the purpose of aggression and death in the playroom. A play therapy session that's focused on helping a child integrate perceived traumatic events (no matter how big or small) is not behavior or social skills training, although children will naturally learn how to manage their behaviors and engage with others through the process this book is suggesting. Our job is to help children learn how to regulate their nervous systems and integrate all the challenging memories, emotions and body sensations that arise as they attempt to play out and understand their perceptions of themselves and their lives.

It's important that we don't shut down the child's need to express whatever they're trying to express. Our job is to help the child find a way to keep the energy moving. This doesn't mean that therapists are punching bags or that we allow whatever happens to happen. The difference in the paradigm is that the boundary is for the therapist. *The moment we think that if the child continues doing whatever he or she is doing and we will have a hard time staying present or become dys-regulated to the point of getting flooded, it's time to set a boundary!*

Boundaries are necessary to keeping us present, because it's our ability to stay present and attuned that creates the container for the energy that's emerging from the aggressive and death play.

Many students have asked me, "When should I set the boundary?" And my answer is, "I have no idea. How can I know when you need it or how big your window of tolerance is in a particular moment? Only you know the answers to those questions."

SETTING BOUNDARIES IS A PERSONAL EXPERIENCE

There are days that my window of tolerance is really big and so is my capacity to stay present in the intensity. There are other days when I don't feel well or something has occurred in my personal life that influences my energy and level of presence. Staying present on some days is definitely easier than it is on others, and I think we need to be honest with ourselves about that.

Our personal history might also be a factor in when we need to set a boundary. If a therapist was hit as a child or witnessed violence and the emotions of those experiences are not fully integrated, it could be more challenging for them to stay present if the child wants to have a sword fight or wants them to witness violent fighting with the toys. The time for therapists to set a boundary is the moment they get a sense that the play is too much for their nervous systems to hold.

We also have physical limitations that can influence when we need to set a boundary. During a play therapy session I had with a young boy while I was pregnant, he wanted to handcuff me to the door so that I'd have to swordfight with one hand and not be able to move around. I knew I wouldn't be able to protect my baby if he swung at my stomach, and I wouldn't be able to focus on the sword fight knowing that my baby wasn't safe, so that was a time for me to set a boundary.

There are many reasons why a boundary might be necessary, but they're all related to helping the therapist stay present.

AM I ENCOURAGING AGGRESSION?

The fear of encouraging aggression is the most common fear that comes up when I teach this new perspective. Therapists fear that if they don't set the boundary when they think they "should," the child will become more aggressive at home or at school. Therapists are afraid that they'll somehow promote the aggressive behavior. What I've found, however, is that when the therapist is authentically using mindfulness, movement and breath and naming their experience out loud to regulate the intensity in the room, it allows children to explore their highly activated dys-regulated states and they begin to develop a sense of awareness regarding their urges, sensations, intensity and emotions. As they move toward their intensity in a more mindful way, the intensity actually begins to dissipate as they become more present and connected with themselves. Rarely does the child become more aggressive at home or at school, but when this does happen, there's usually something else going on in the environment that the child is continuing to perceive as a high threat or challenge.

On the other hand, when therapists act or role-play and don't name their authentic experience while regulating the intensity, children typically amp up the play until they get an authentic response. Although there's a discharge, it doesn't necessarily mean that the energy is being integrated or that the child is developing a strong sense of awareness of their sensations and emotions. This is what leads to the potential for more acting-out behaviors outside the therapy sessions. Don't underestimate the power of your authentic presence.

EMPHASIZING AND REDIRECTING

Based on this new paradigm, we set boundaries to help us to stay present and set them the moment we can't stay in our own window of tolerance for whatever reason. So, how do we do it? What does setting a boundary look like?

First, we want to keep in mind that we're not trying to stop the energy (this is what our fear response wants us to do). We're trying to redirect it in such a way that we can stay present and continue to allow children to explore the emotions and sensations that are arising. We want to keep them engaged in the play without triggering their brains' perception of us as a threat.

Let's explore a few scenarios and discuss them from the child's perspective:

Scenario 1

In the story of Sarah and her therapist at the beginning of this chapter, when the therapist stopped the play and told Sarah it wasn't okay to handcuff him, Sarah stopped and was confused. Why?

Sarah's brain most likely experienced two things: incongruence in the environment and a "should," or in this case a "shouldn't." Her brain might have been thinking, "If there are handcuffs in here, why wouldn't I be allowed to put them on you? Isn't that what they're for? If not, why are they in here?"

Scenario 2

You're engaged in an intense moment of play with four-year-old Ben and he's shouting, stabbing at you and coming at you from every direction. Suddenly, you know you've had it. "Okay, you know what? That's too much," you say. "We can't play like that in here."

Ben's brain has a high probability of registering this as a threat because of the confusion and the abrupt nature of the boundary-setting. Ben is stopped in the middle of his expression and given the message that his expression is not okay. He will probably experience an internal conflict between what his nervous system needs to do and what he's told he can't do. In all probability, this is the same message he gets outside the playroom when he becomes hyper-aroused and sets others up to feel overwhelmed.

Scenario 3

You're sword-fighting with nine-year-old Sally and she catches you off guard and hits you pretty hard. Your buttons get pushed and you say sternly, "So, there's a rule in here that therapists aren't for hurting. You can't hurt me."

Sally's brain will most likely register this as a threat because she's receiving a "shouldn't" message. She might also be confused by the incongruence of the therapist's engaging in a sword fight but then saying that therapists aren't for hurting. People sometimes get hurt in sword fights.

Another consideration is that when therapists set rules like "You can't hurt me" in the context of trauma work, they're inadvertently telling the child that in that moment, he or she is a perpetrator. The therapist has just made the child the bad guy in the room and turned the aggression into a personal experience, rather than remembering that this is all part of the setup and finding another way to set the boundary.

When setting boundaries based on a should or a shouldn't or out of fear, consider that the child has probably experienced some version of this in life and may still be experiencing it. The child tries to express his or her hyper-aroused state and most likely gets feedback such as "Stop. Contain. Calm down. You're too much." Consider the possibility that when we abruptly stop the play and say no, what we're doing is reinforcing that it isn't okay to express certain feeling and reinforcing the brain wiring that supports that story, too.

It's not uncommon for children to amp it up when they feel shamed, controlled or threatened by a boundary. I've witnessed countless interactions where, as soon as the therapist sets a boundary, the child does everything he or she can to regain a sense of control over the therapist. In a nutshell, children will set therapists up to feel what having the boundary set just felt like to them.

KEEPING THE FLOW: EMPATHIZE AND REDIRECT

Now lets explore a few examples of how to set boundaries while keeping the energy moving and staying connected to the child.

Example 1:

You're having a fast-paced sword fight with six-year-old Shawn and he's swinging at your head and you're starting to feel overwhelmed. It's just too much and you don't think you can stay present much longer if he keeps swinging at your head. As you're fighting, you look him in the eye and, reverting to your normal tone of voice, say, "Shawn, hit me from here down," as you gesture toward everything below your head.

Example 2:

Eight-year-old Janet is stabbing you and yelling at you. You're beginning to feel disoriented and are having a hard time regulating. She drops the sword, walks over to the sand tray and starts dumping the sand out onto the floor. You feel a strong need to control and stop her arise in your body, signaling to you that it's time to set a boundary. You make eye contact with her and, changing your voice so that it's different from the voice you've been using, say, "Janet, this is so important for you to do. The sand needs to come out." You grab a shower curtain and quickly put it on the floor and invite her to continue dumping the sand onto the shower curtain. You are once again able to be present and help facilitate her process.

Example 3:

Three-year-old Tyler grabs a scoop of sand and lunges toward you, trying to put sand in your mouth and eyes. You look Tyler in the eye and, changing your voice, say, "Show me another way." Tyler says, "No ... In mouth" You look him in the eye again, get present and say, "Tyler, this is so important to you. You need the sand to go on a face and in a mouth. Show me with a different face and mouth." (You'd have to get more specific, since he's three and in the midst of enacting a trauma memory.) He walks to the shelf and grabs a baby doll, puts her on the floor and proceeds to pour the sand into her eyes and mouth.

In all three of these examples, the children felt understood. They also felt respected, which is very important. The majority of children will shift and find another way when the boundary is set in this way, because the truth is that they want to play with you and they want you to understand. When you're able to stay in attunement with the child as you set the boundary, you allow the child's nervous system to continue to do what it needs to do.

There will be a few children who won't show you another way right away, and you might have to say it a few times. If this occurs, get curious about the following details:

1.   Did I make eye contact?
2.   Did I say the child's name?

3. Did I change the tone of my voice so that they child knew I was no longer playing?

4. Did I say, "Show me another way"? Or did I ask the child, "Can you show me another way?" When you ask, the child gets to say no.

5. Was I present so that the child could *feel* me?

Children really need to know that you understand and that you're not trying to control or stop the play. Most important, they need to *feel* you and your respect. Setting boundaries in this way in the midst of the play teaches children about listening, empathy and respecting the needs of another. The message the therapist is delivering is "Let's meet in the middle and I'm going to take care of myself" rather than "You have to stop because I'm uncomfortable." What a beautiful lesson in relationship to have modeled to the child.

THE REPAIR

Sometimes, doing what you can to regulate yourself will not be enough. It's inevitable that even after practicing what you learn in this book, you'll have a session that's so intense and overwhelming that you'll go past your own window of tolerance and become highly dys-regulated. You're human, remember. In these moments, you'll most likely set a boundary out of fear and it will register in the child's mind as abrupt, controlling and possibly even shaming. If and when this happens, know that you're not the only one. I have yet to meet a play therapist who hasn't done this. The beautiful part about this is that when we have a very human moment, we get to do the repair. I love repairs because the modeling that occurs for a child is so profound and priceless.

Take a moment and imagine or recall setting a boundary out of fear and becoming angry and stern with a child. As soon as you realize that you set your boundary out of fear and that you didn't quite handle it the way you wanted to, you have a chance to do repair work right away in the session or at the next session. For example, at the beginning of your next session with the child, imagine saying something like, "Joey, remember last time when we were playing and I got mad all of a sudden and told you to stop and that it wasn't okay to play like that? I realized that my brain got really scared and that's why I said what I said. I also realized that I didn't do enough things to take care of myself like breathing, moving and telling you how I was feeling, so when I got scared, I got scared fast! What I really wanted to say but couldn't find the words was, 'Show me another way.' So if you decide today that you would like to play like that again and I need to take care of myself, this time I will just ask you to show me another way so that we can keep playing. Playing with you is really important to me."

What does this teach the child?

1. It's okay to be human.
2. When we do something that we know affects another person, take responsibility.
3. Try again

As your window of tolerance expands, you'll probably feel comfortable setting fewer boundaries, and the types of boundaries you'll need will tend to change.

In Chapter 7, we'll look at hyper-arousal and how we can effectively work with that energy

CHAPTER 6 KEY POINTS

- Therapists often struggle with an internal conflict the moment we think a boundary might be necessary. If we set a boundary because we think we're "supposed to" or "should," we might not feel confident in our decision and question ourselves afterward.

- If we're clear about why we're setting the boundary, we can do it in a way that doesn't cause us or the child to feel shame. Empathize and redirect instead of saying no.

- When setting a boundary, it's important that we still get to be ourselves and so does the child.

- Kids don't need boundaries in the playroom—therapists do!

- A play therapy session that's focused on helping a child integrate perceived traumatic events (no matter how big or small) is not behavior or social skills training.

- It's important that we don't shut down the child's need to express whatever he or she is trying to express.

- The moment we think that if the child continues doing what he or she is doing we'll have a hard time staying present or become dys-regulated to the point of getting flooded, it's time to set a boundary!

- Boundaries are necessary to keeping us present, because it's our ability to stay present and attuned that creates the container for the energy that's emerging from the aggressive and death play.

- When we set a boundary, we're not trying to stop the energy—we're trying to redirect it in such a way that we can remain present and continue to allow children to explore the emotions and sensations that are arising. We want to keep them engaged in the play without triggering their brains' perception of us as a threat.

- It's imperative for us to remember that whatever the child is doing is part of the setup and that we must set boundaries in a way that doesn't make the child the bad guy in the room.

- When we abruptly stop the play and say no, we're reinforcing that it isn't okay to express certain feeling and reinforcing the brain wiring that supports that story.

- It's not uncommon for children to amp it up when they feel shamed, controlled or threatened by a boundary.

- When children feel understood and respected by the way we set a boundary, they will usually find another way to express what they want you to feel, because they want to play with us and want us to understand.

- When we stay in attunement with the child as we set the boundary, we allow the child's nervous system to continue to do what it needs to do.

CHAPTER 7

Hyper-Aroused Play

Scott, age seven, put the blocks away and sat beside me on the floor, and I felt a strange anxiety enter my body. I noticed that my breathing was changing. I noticed that the energy in the room had changed, almost as if the room were holding its breath. Just as I registered these changes, he grabbed a snake puppet and threw it at me. Imagining that it was a real snake on top of me, I shrieked and quickly tried to push it off. And then I took a deep breath, allowing the shock to release from my body. Next a spider came at me and then a dragon

107

and then a shark. I was confused. I was scared. I spontaneously said things like "I don't understand why this is happening. I'm scared. I have no protection."

As I attempted to ground the energy through regulation, I rubbed my legs, moved my feet, put one hand on my heart and the other on my belly to help myself breathe, and, when possible, taking deep breaths, focusing on my exhale to let the energy go. I allowed the experience to feel real while holding the knowledge that it wasn't real. I stayed present and used mindfulness to expand my window of tolerance to hold the intensity. I used movement and breath and named my experience to regulate the energy in my nervous system.

Scott had been a witness to domestic violence, and he set me up to feel his world. He helped me understand what if feels like to be hypervigilant. In our play, I felt scared that I'd get hurt, but I never actually got hurt. He never made the animals bite me. The stress of being on constant alert for being injured, increased the tension throughout my body and was confusing to my mind. Scott was giving me a window into his world.

Before we discuss hyper-arousal in the playroom, I want you to take a moment and refer back to the nervous system chart in Chapter 2 to refresh yourself with the symptoms of hyper-arousal. Aggressive play is the symbolic form of the hyper-aroused state of the nervous system. When a child is playing, his associated memories and feelings will arise. If what he's recalling is not integrated, he'll feel the symptoms of dys-regulation in his body. When his nervous system gets activated into a hyper-aroused state, there's a good chance that intense play will enter the playroom. Remember that if we don't regulate during intense play, *we risk increasing the intensity* in the play because the child is attempting to get us to have an authentic response, and we also risk experiencing vicarious trauma and compassion fatigue. *Our ability to stay present is the container for the intensity that arises in the playroom.*

REGULATING THROUGH HYPER-AROUSAL/AGGRESSION

Breathe!

Holding our breath is a natural response when we're scared or we feel intensity in our bodies. I've observed many therapists in the midst of the aggressive play holding their breath or breathing in a very shallow way. What this does is intensify the experience, contribute to hyperventilation and fatigue and keep the hyper-aroused energy at high intensity levels.

Remember, the goal here is to move toward the intensity, and to do this we must be open to feeling the intensity in a mindful way. One of the ways we can facilitate moving toward the intensity is through our breath. It sounds simple, but becoming conscious of our breathing in the midst of the intensity helps us remain regulated so that we can integrate the experience.

As we begin to experience the hyper-aroused energy in the room and our breathing becomes faster and more shallow, it's important to elongate our exhale to ground and release the energy. Sometimes the play is happening so quickly, like in a sword fight, that it's hard to take a deep breath. In these moments, I remind myself to take a deep breath between the hits and swings.

Use your breath to help regulate your nervous system in the midst of the aggression so that you can stay present in the intensity.

Be Vocal!

If you have a sword coming at your head or you're watching a doll being hit or thrown onto the floor, this is not the time to be quiet (unless you've been set up to have no voice or are silenced in some way in the play). This is the time to share your experience out loud by describing what it's like for you to observe the aggression. This is the time to be real! In doing so, you may find yourself screaming or saying things like "I'm scared," "I don't know how to protect myself," "Ouch!" "I don't even understand why I'm fighting" or maybe even "Why is this happening to me? I'm worried about the baby." There isn't a "right" thing to say in the midst of the intensity. Whatever is true for you in the moment is what's important to vocalize.

And it's just as important to make observational statements about what the child is literally doing (this is explored in detail in the next chapter) as it is to share our own experience out loud in the play.

Work With the Energy in the Room

I want you to imagine that you're a martial artist and that an opponent is coming at you. What do you do? Do you stop the opponent by saying, "No, you can't do that"? Do you walk away? No, you move toward the opponent mindfully.

When your opponent strikes, you don't move away from the strike. Instead you meet it. You allow yourself to be present with the intensity and then you let it go. And then the next strike comes. You meet it, you're present with it and you let it go.

We can see the same process in yoga when we face a challenge. Maybe you hit a place of tightness in your body or are about to lose your balance. What do you do? You lean in toward the challenge mindfully, being present with the sensations, and then, using your breath, you release, letting go into the pose.

The point is, when we're playing with our clients, we have to mindfully and authentically feel the experience but not become completely absorbed in the experience. As the child's intensity comes toward us, we practice being present with ourselves and with the energy itself. We practice allowing ourselves to feel the setup and the intensity. We give ourselves permission to have an authentic reaction to whatever is occurring, and then we let it all go. We can repeat this with each wave of intensity that comes toward us.

The session I had with four-year-old Henry illustrates this practice. I was smashed between my chair and my couch, curled up to protect myself while Henry hissed at me and threw burning poison on me. I was oscillating between screaming and barely being able to get the words out as the poison covered my body. "My body is hurting," "Ouch," "It's on fire!" "Make it stop!" "I can't breathe," "I'm scared," "I don't trust", "It isn't safe"—those were some of the things I said. He came at me again, hissing in my face in a primal animalistic way, and my body tightened from the fear. Allowing myself to stay present in the experience but not be consumed by it, I silently reminded myself that I was in a play therapy session. I breathed. I breathed a lot. I focused on the exhale of my breath to allow for some release to occur as I was being set up to feel incredible pain and sensations of terror. I wiggled my toes because they were the only parts of my body I could move. I felt the intensity and then let it go. I came back to myself. And then Henry came at me again, hissing and this time pressing a pillow against me, creating more pressure. I was enveloped in overwhelm, pain and terror and unable to do anything to make it stop. And once again, I allowed myself to *feel it, name it, move it and let it go.*

LET'S SWORD-FIGHT!

Whether it was playing cowboys and Indians or cops and robbers or having pillow fights as children, most of us have experienced the energy of a play fight. And typically we were laughing, fighting back equally hard, being competitive and silly and playful. Although the energy in a sword fight in the playroom is familiar, the way to make it therapeutic is very different.

Here are some tips for facilitating sword fights in the playroom. Keep in mind that these are general guidelines and not rules. If children need something different to occur, they'll let you know. Most important, trust your intuition.

Don't Win—Lose Your Power Slowly

Just like in other forms of play, in sword fights children are attempting to set you up to feel how they feel, which typically is powerless. They're coming in feeling disempowered and struggling to integrate their perception of a challenge that they're experiencing or have experienced.

It's important to lose your power. Let yourself feel what it's like to feel helpless because you don't have enough power, you're not strong enough and you can't protect yourself well.

A great way to help you lose your power is to get yourself backed into a corner or a couch so that you can slowly fall to the floor or onto the couch, becoming smaller and smaller.

Don't Be Too Good

Children need a worthy opponent, but if you're *too* good, the fight becomes more about defeating you as the therapist, not to mention that the children have to work really hard. It's also important to get down to their height level as best you can and sword-fight from there.

I saw a great example of a therapist being too good a sword fighter during one of our Synergetic Intensive trainings. The therapist was a tall woman and her client was a five-year-old boy half her size. As he began the sword fight, she remained standing tall and swung her sword high above his head. The result was that the child couldn't take her power away easily. He was jumping and swinging up high to try to get her sword. He tried everything he could think of to get her to go down, which is where he needed her to be in order for her to feel helpless and powerless. He tried to stab her, he fought with two swords, he even pulled up a chair to stand on, but nothing worked. In the end, he took his sword and swiped her legs to "cut them off" and she finally got the message and went down.

Do I Fight Back?

Whether you fight back depends on a number of factors. I've been in sword fights where the sword was coming at me so strong and fast that I couldn't fight back even if I wanted to! Other times the child will go slow and then speed it up, lunging at you and teasing you. You may get your arms cut off immediately and have no protection. There are so many variations, but what matters most is the context and the energy that's arising as a result of how the sword fight is playing out.

If you're able to fight back, then, of course, fight back if that's what seems authentic, but follow these two important guidelines:

- Don't hit the child with the sword on purpose unless instructed to do so.
- If the child tells you to hit him with the sword, do it very

carefully and have the child dictate exactly what you're supposed to do. It's critical that the child script these moments in the play.

I've observed that therapists who have a high need for control or who don't like the feeling of losing or being powerless will sometimes get in a little jab. Maybe it's a quick little hit to the child's leg when there's a lull in the energy or a quick little stab when they aren't looking. Sometimes it's hard to lose our power and we want a moment of feeling powerful. If this arises in the playroom, acknowledge your need to yourself, breathe and then give yourself permission to feel the uncomfortable feelings you're trying to avoid.

Scripting the Play

When children ask you to hit them with your sword (or shoot them or handcuff them or anything else that seems aggressive), it's extremely important that the children are able to script what follows. This is typically a time in the therapy process when children need you to become the challenge so that they can empower themselves. When this happens, pause and ask the child to tell you exactly how to do it.

For example, when Jennifer, age eight, and I were sword-fighting, she had two swords and a shield and I had nothing. I was being set up to feel completely powerless, frozen in fear and with absolutely no way to protect myself. All of a sudden, she handed me her swords and shield. "Now you get me," she said. I paused for a moment and became present. "Do you want me to do it exactly how you did it to me or in another way?" I asked. "Just like I did to you," she said. As I approached her to begin the sword fight, I remained mindful of my breathing and was *careful not to do anything that I hadn't seen her do before.* Just as I was about to swing at her legs, she threw a magic potion on me that turned me into a statue, reclaiming her power.

In the next chapter, we'll look at how to use regulation when we're observing aggressive or death play.

CHAPTER 7 KEY POINTS

- Regulate, regulate, regulate.
- Aggressive play is the symbolic form of the hyper-aroused state of the nervous system.
- Our ability to remain present is the container for the intensity that arises in the playroom.
- Holding our breath or breathing in a very shallow way intensifies the experience, contributes to hyperventilation and fatigue and keeps the hyper-aroused energy at high intensity levels.
- As we begin to experience the hyper-aroused energy in the room and our breathing becomes faster and more shallow, it's important to elongate our exhale to ground and release the energy.
- If we have a sword coming at our head or we're watching a doll being hit or thrown onto the floor, we need to be real and share our experience out loud by describing what it's like for us to observe the aggression.
- When we're playing with our clients, we have to mindfully and authentically feel the experience but not become completely absorbed in the experience.
- Feel it, name it, move it and let it go.
- Trust your intuition.

- Just like in other forms of play, in sword fights children are attempting to set you up to feel how they feel, which typically is powerless. They're coming in feeling disempowered and struggling to integrate their perception of a challenge they're experiencing or have experienced.

- When children ask you to hit them with your sword (or shoot them or handcuff them or anything else that seems aggressive), it's extremely important that the children are able to script what follows.

- When Sword-Fighting:
  - ◊ Don't win—lose your power slowly.
  - ◊ Get down on the child's level.
  - ◊ Don't be *too* good.
  - ◊ Don't hit the child with the sword on purpose unless instructed to do so.
  - ◊ If the child tells you to hit him with the sword, do it very carefully and have the child dictate exactly what you're supposed to do. It's critical that the child script these moments in the play.

CHAPTER 8

Observing Play

Have you ever watched something in a session that was highly aggressive or filled with death? Have you ever had to sit there while a child played out a highly intense scene that left your nervous system highly activated in a state of hyper-arousal? Have you ever watched something so intense that you found yourself wanting to check out or numb out as hypo-arousal set in? Being set up as the observer is a common role for play therapists, either because the child sets the play up that way or because the style of play therapy being used is observational in nature.

We might have to watch a war between the army men or a scary scene set in a dollhouse where someone gets significantly hurt. We might have to watch a baby doll be thrown around the room. We might have to watch the child beat up the bop bag, puppets attack each other or a small animal toy be shot at. It doesn't matter if you're watching or directly in the play, you're going to feel the intensity whether you consciously register it or not. Therefore, it's vitally important to practice regulating your own nervous system so that you don't walk out of your session with the symptoms of having just witnessed violence, which you did!

Observing aggressive and death play without understanding the importance of self-regulation for yourself and for your child client is one of the fastest ways to increase the potential for burnout. It's also one of the fastest ways to create symptoms of dys-regulation in your own system that stay with you long after the session is over.

Everything you've learned in this book is just as applicable when you're observing as it is when you're participating. You're still working toward authentic expression and modeling self-regulation through mindfulness, movement, breath and naming your experience out loud. The child is still observing how you manage the intensity of the emotions and sensations that are arising. You're still helping to rewire children's neural networks as they move toward their dys-regulated states with awareness while trying the regulation techniques they've been observing you using.

THE SIGNIFICANCE OF THE OBSERVER

For those of you who use a play therapy style that allows the child to choose whether you'll be an active participant in the play or watch the play, have you ever considered the possibility that being placed in the observer role isn't random? What if I told you that when a child chooses to put you in the observer role, that's also part of the setup?

Consider these scenarios: Toby witnessed domestic violence between his parents; Sheila was forced to watch her sibling be sexually violated; Max saw his mom killed in a car accident; Leila walked into her living room and found her mom passed out on the floor after drinking too much. How would these children help you understand what it felt like to be them? One of the ways is by making you an observer.

So if you use a style of play therapy that naturally puts you in the observer role, you aren't off the hook—the setup is still taking place. The child will still do whatever it takes to help you understand what it feels like to be him or her, and your nervous system will still be affected by the intensity.

HOW TO BE AN OBSERVER

One of the biggest considerations is that what you say has to make sense. For example, if the child is hurting the baby doll and the therapist is crying as if he or she is the baby, the child will probably wonder or say, "You're not hurting. Why are you crying? The baby's down there. You're fine." Kids will stop in the middle of the play because they're confused and momentarily disoriented by the incongruency. It's confusing to them because it doesn't make sense. And we know that when something doesn't make sense in the environment, the child's brain will pause and orient toward the confusion to try to figure it out. When this happens, children get pulled out of their experience and into their analytical thinking as they try to make sense of the incongruency. Our goal is to have the child spend as much time in self-reflection as possible, and making statements that make sense facilitates this. Here are three types of congruent reflections that are important to include:

1. Observational Statements

Observational statements are an important part of the play therapy process because they let children know that we're with them and *tracking them*. Observational statements describe what the therapist is observing. Examples include:

- The cars are crashing into each other.
- There's a monster in the house (watching the child play with a monster in a dollhouse).
- Superman and Batman are fighting each other (watching the child making the superheroes hit each other).

These types of statements also have a regulatory effect for you as the therapist because they help you oscillate between the intensity of your inner experience and the experience you're observing. Being able to use self-reflective statements and statements that describe what you're noticing the child do is great modeling for the child because the child gets to witness the therapist using mindfulness to be aware of *self and other,* a significant part of the attachment process. When you make observational statements, be sure to simply state the obvious, without interpretation. "Just the facts, just the facts," I tell my students.

2. Authentic Experience as the Observer

As the observer, it's important that you vocalize what it's like to be the observer. What does it feel like to have to watch whatever it is you're being asked to watch? Are you nervous? Do you feel helpless? Does your stomach hurt? Are you confused? Are you scared? If you're watching a fight, do you know why the fighting is happening?

When the child sets you up as the observer, it's because he or she needs you to feel what it's like to observe and not be able to do anything about what's occurring. I find this to be especially common among children who have witnessed domestic violence. If therapists aren't willing to say what it feels like to observe the fighting, they're potentially missing a huge piece of the experience.

Let's consider the following session. Lonnie, who is four years old, placed a baby doll on the couch and told the therapist that the baby was drowning. The therapist immediately began to express her fear, helplessness and terror as she stood there watching the baby drown. "The baby! Help! No one is helping the baby! I'm scared! I want to save the baby!" She was also regulating through the intensity as she shook her arms, rocked back and forth and put her hand on her chest to support her breathing. Lonnie had watched his younger brother drown when he was two years old and couldn't do anything to save him. He needed the therapist to understand, and so he set her up to observe a baby drowning. As they played through this event, Lonnie's own nervous system moved from a freeze response toward mobilization as he observed his therapist attuning to him and modeling self-regulation. In the midst of the intensity, he began to modulate the energy in his own nervous system by taking deep breaths and moving alongside the therapist.

3. *Voicing the Toy*

The last type of reflection for observers is to voice what the toy is feeling. Again, it's very important for the therapist to make sense here. We don't want the child to spend time trying to figure the therapist out. We want the therapist's reflections to help deepen children's play experience and understanding of themselves. One of the easiest ways to do this is to make statements that sound like "If I were the (name the toy), I would be feeling ..." or "If I were the (name the toy), I would be thinking..." With these types of statements, the therapist is staying congruent and the child doesn't have to spend time trying to make sense of what the therapist just said. In the example of the crying baby that appeared earlier in this chapter, the therapist could say, "If I were the baby, I would be hurting and crying," and then cry as if she were the baby. The therapist could also use the other types of reflections to help deepen the play while still being congruent.

Questions to Ask Yourself

- Does what I'm saying make sense?
- Am I being authentic?
- Am I being congruent with what I am experiencing and expressing?

USING THE BOP BAG

Some therapists believe that using bop bags promotes aggression in children, while others believe it's essential toy to the playroom, allowing the child to express himself fully and thus encouraging empowerment.

In an effort to bridge these opinions, let's explore how to use the bop bag in ways that avoid promoting aggression while encouraging the child to understand his or her need to express aggression. Please note that the examples listed below are just examples. There are many possibilities that are effective for deepening children's awareness of themselves when they use a bop bag. Follow your intuition and trust your experience. It's also important to note that the bop bag is a versatile toy and is not limited to one type of use in the playroom. Although most children will use the bop bag as a way to project their feelings of disempowerment or empowerment, other children will use it as a source of comfort, leaning and resting on it for support, or as a sensory toy, bouncing and rolling on it to help regulate their nervous systems (these are just two examples of other ways a bop bag can be used).

Here are a few key guidelines to follow when a child chooses to use the bop bag:

- Don't assume you know who or what the child wants the bop bag to represent. It's not important for you to know.

- Unless you know the intended gender of the bop bag, it's best to refer to the bop bag as "it."

- Make reflections that address the underlying feelings the child is attempting to project onto the bop bag. Example: The child picks up the bop bag and starts throwing it around the room, turning it upside down and making it spin quickly, and you're having to get out of the way to protect yourself.

Here are some examples of effective responses:

◊ Voice the bop bag: "If I were it/him/her, I'd be thinking, 'I'm spinning out of control. My world is upside down.'"

◊ Voice what it's like to be the observer: "I am scared and nervous watching this. I have to protect myself. I'm starting to feel out of control."

◊ Voice your observation of the bop bag: "Its world is turned upside and it has no control."

◊ Voice your observation of the child's interaction with the bop bag: "You want it/him to know what it feels like to have everything upside down and have no control."

- As much as possible, avoid reflections that encourage aggression. Examples of reflections that encourage aggression are "Get him," "You are so strong," "Show him how mad you are," "Hit him again." These types of statements promote aggression.

- If children choose to use the bop bag for support or a way to regulate, provide reflections that enhance their awareness of what they're doing. Example: a child has been running around the room in an anxious/frantic way, going from toy to toy. He finds the bop bag and lies on top of it, struggling to gain his balance. Here are some examples of effective responses:

  ◊ Voice your observation of the bop bag: "It keeps moving. It's hard for it/him/her to keep steady and support you."

  ◊ Voice your observation of the child's interaction with the bop bag: "You're trying so hard to make it stop moving so that you can relax on top. It's so hard to find a way to relax when things just keeps moving."

- Match the intensity of the play. The child will keep turning the play up until the therapist embodies/names the intensity.

- The most important principal to be aware of when the child works with the bop bag in an aggressive way is that your ability to stay present and connected to yourself and to the child during the high level of intensity is the most healing aspect of the experience. If the child becomes highly dys-regulated and his aggression escalates, it's your ability to stay regulated and emotionally/energetically present that will ground the child.

The general guidelines for working with a child and a bop bag are essentially the same no matter what toy the child is choosing to play with.

In the next chapter, we'll look at hypo-arousal and explore why death play can be so therapeutic.

CHAPTER 8 KEY POINTS

- Being set up as the observer is a common role for play therapists either because the child sets the play up that way or because the style of play therapy being used is observational in nature.

- Whether we're watching aggressive play or we're in it, we feel the intensity even if we don't consciously register it, so it's vitally important to practice regulating our own nervous systems.

- Observing aggressive and death play without understanding the importance of self-regulation for yourself and for your child client is one of the fastest ways to increase the potential for burnout. It's also one of the fastest ways to create symptoms of dys-regulation in your own system that stay with you long after the session is over.

- When we're observing play, what we say has to make sense.

- Observational statements are an important part of the play therapy process because they let children know we're with them and *tracking them.*

- Using self-reflective statements describing what we're experiencing and statements that describe what the child is doing is great modeling for the child because he gets to witness us using mindfulness to be aware of *self and other*, a significant part of the attachment process.

- When we make observational statements, we can simply state the obvious, without interpretation.

- As the observer, it's important that you vocalize what it's like to be the observer.

- We have to make sense when we voice the toys the child is playing with so that the child doesn't have to spend time trying to figure us out.

- The bop bag is a versatile toy and is not limited to one type of use in the playroom.

- Questions to Ask Yourself

   ◊ Does what I'm saying make sense?

   ◊ Am I being authentic?

   ◊ Am I being congruent with what I am experiencing and expressing?

CHAPTER 9

Hypo-Aroused Play

walk into the waiting room to greet five-year-old Jenny, who is sitting next to her mom. I lean down to say hello and Jenny bolts out of her chair and runs down the hallway. I'm so stunned that there isn't time to register my feelings. I turn and run after her. As I try to catch up, I see her run into my playroom. Just as I cross the threshold of the playroom door, Jenny pulls out a toy gun and shoots me. I'm dead and remain that way for the rest of the session.

All I could think was, "I didn't even get to say hi." I felt incredibly sad, abandoned, rejected and lonely.

IS DEATH IN THE PLAYROOM REALLY NECESSARY?

Jenny was adopted at birth. In many ways, she had the pic-ture-perfect adoption story. Her birth mother was a high-functioning sixteen-year-old from a good home who decided that she wasn't ready to be a mother. After she made the deci-sion to place Jenny for adoption, she handpicked the adoptive parents. Jenny's adoptive parents were involved during the en-tire pregnancy and were also in the room at the time of the delivery. When Jenny emerged into the world, she was placed into her adoptive mother's arms.

She had to kill me because I had to know what it felt like to want to say hello and connect and to then feel completely abandoned, rejected and not wanted. I needed to understand the level of abandonment and shock that she experienced.

With death as the symbolic representation in play of the hypo-aroused state of the nervous system, it's a very important state to explore. Children who are experiencing a degree of emotional numbing, dissociation, emotional constriction and depression often present in a hypo-aroused state. Remember from Chapter 2 that when we perceive a challenge that's so big that we think we can't do anything about it or it's gone on too long or is too intense, the nervous system naturally goes into a hypo-aroused state for the sake of self-preservation. For children who are having this experience, death play may be a very important part of the therapy. Death can also be used as part of the setup to let the therapist know what it feels like to be helpless, unimportant and deeply rejected and even want to just disappear. Death play may also be literal for some children who have witnessed a death or experienced the loss of a loved one.

Therapists have fears about whether playing with death promotes death. They are often afraid that if they play dead or allow death to occur, they're promoting scary behavior outside the playroom. It's important to remember that just like in aggressive play, the therapist's ability to stay present, regulate and model mindfulness in the midst of the intensity helps promote integration. When the therapist is checking out, not naming the intensity of the emotions that are arising in the play and not present with what's occurring in her body and in the relationship with the child, she takes the risk that the child will need to take the play outside the room to continue the attempts at integration.

FALLING TO YOUR DEATH

Over the years through much trial and error, some comical and some painful, I've learned that there is indeed a helpful way to fall when you die. *It's important to die in a way that protects you from being hurt and allows you to maintain knowl-edge of what's happening in the room with the child.* It's also important to stay dead until you are told you're alive again or until the session is over.

In one session, I was told that I was a robber and had to try to rob the bank. As I sneaked toward the cash register, Margaret called out for me to turn toward her and put my hands in the air. I put my hands in the air, and as I turned around, she shot me. I stumbled back and she shot me again. My body responded as if I were really being shot. Recognizing that I was probably dead at this point, I fell. Unfortunately, I didn't plan my fall, and as I fell backward, my back went right into the corner of the sand tray. Ouch. I landed on my back completely exposed with my arms out wide. Next thing I knew she was stabbing a sword into my gut. Ouch again.

Here are some suggestions for keeping yourself safe when you need to die in the playroom:

- Fall onto something soft. If you're shot, stabbed or pretend-punched, you can always stumble back into or onto something comfy like a couch or a chair.
- When you fall, make sure you fall in a way that protects your head and stomach. Curl up if possible. If you fall onto your back with your stomach and heart exposed,

you have a high probability of being shot or stabbed there. Trust me!

- Don't fully close your eyes. If you do, you'll feel very vulnerable, which can induce feelings of hypervigilance. You also won't be able to track the child. It's okay to have your eyes open and stare into the distance. With your eyes open, you can use your peripheral vision to see what's happening.

- Make sure that however you fall, you fall facing the center of the room so that your back isn't turned away from what the child is doing.

- If you have to fall to the floor, fall into fetal position. Land in a position where you're resting your head on one extended arm for support while placing the other over the top of your head. In doing so, you'll create a gap between your arms that you can peek through.

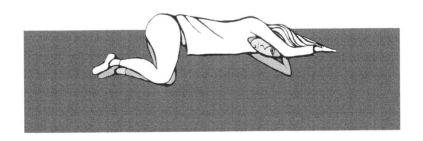

DEAD PEOPLE DON'T TALK

When therapists die, it's important that they don't talk. I've seen therapists repeatedly attempt to talk while they're dead, and each time they were killed again. Talking while dead actually prolongs the process. I've also noticed that the desire to talk while dead typically comes from a therapist's desire to not have to feel everything he or she is feeling while dead. Many times it's also a way for the therapist to reestablish a sense of being in control, because—let's be honest—playing dead is a very helpless and out-of-control experience.

There are three exceptions to the rule against talking while dead:

- If the children are young and a lot of time goes by, it's important to remind them that they're in charge and can make you come alive when they want you to. You can sit up quickly and whisper, "You're in charge and can make me be alive whenever you want," and then lie back down.

- Just because you're dead doesn't mean you don't have to be aware of time. It's still important to tell the children they have ten minutes left or five minutes or one minute. *It's still important to track time even if you're dead.*

- Being dead doesn't mean you can no longer set boundaries

when you need to. If you're dead and the child is continuing to stab you or tries to hurt you, it's important that you give yourself permission to set a boundary. You can refer back to Chapter 6 for more information on setting boundaries. *It's still important to set boundaries even if you're dead.*

REGULATING THROUGH HYPO-AROUSAL AND DEATH

Playing dead can be just as intense as aggressive play, if not more so. Hypo-arousal regulation can be challenging because there isn't a lot of energy to work with, but it's essential to continue to use mindfulness, breath, movement and naming your experience out loud (when you're allowed to talk) as part of the process. If you don't, you will experience high levels of numbing, potentially check out and dissociate. You're still registering the intensity on some level, and without regulation you'll probably feel the effects of the play sometime after the session.

Probably the most challenging part of facilitating hypo-aroused energy in death play is that when you're dead, you're not able to talk and you have to be still. For these reasons, *regulation has to become an internal process.* Even though you can't name your experience out loud or move outwardly, you can use mindfulness, breath and internal movements to help facilitate the dys-regulation in your nervous system and remain present.

Even though you're dead, you still have a body! While you're lying there, remind yourself that you're not really dead and that it's still important to practice regulation through the intense sensations you might be experiencing. Here are some tips for regulating your body.

Breathe, breathe, breathe.

One of the best ways to regulate yourself and keep yourself present is through regulated breathing. In Chapter 4, we discussed how our breathing patterns can create states of dys-regulation in our nervous system and how by regulating your breathing, you can help your nervous system become less activated.

While you're dead, practice regulated breathing. This is especially helpful when you have to be dead for an extended period of time. You regulate your breathing by making your inhalation and your exhalation the same length of time. Sometimes it's even helpful to silently count during the breaths. As you breathe in, slowly count one-two-three-four, and as you breathe out, slowly count one-two-three-four. Continue to repeat the cycle. It doesn't matter what number you count to as long as it feels comfortable to you.

Reflection: Lie on the floor as if you're dead and practice regulated breathing for one minute.

Do body scans.

Another strategy for keeping yourself present is a body scan. Using mindfulness, place your attention on your feet, pausing to notice them. You may find that they feel quite active inside, or you may notice that you can't feel them. Just notice. Then turn your attention to other parts of your body, each time pausing and noticing how they feel.

As you notice parts of your body, you may want to move them. If this is the case, find ways of moving that aren't visible to the child. Wiggling your toes in your shoes, tightening and releasing your muscles and pressing your body into the floor or couch are some ways you can bring subtle movement into death play. For optimal regulation, you might even consider doing movements that are bilaterally oriented (*bilateral* means "affecting both sides"). For example, alternately tighten the muscles in your left leg and your right leg. This activates both the right and left hemispheres of your brain, promoting integration.

YOU STILL HAVE FEELINGS!

Even though you're dead, you're being set up to feel the child's perception of himself and the challenging experiences he's gone through. As you're lying there, ask yourself, "How am I feeling right now? Do I feel lonely? Do I feel sad? Do I feel helpless? Did I never even have a chance for survival? Do I feel unimportant? Do I feel relief because I don't want to deal with the intensity of hyper-arousal or aggression anymore?" (The last question reflects a common feeling when death occurs after a period of high-intensity aggressive play.)

Even though you can't say these things out loud, you're acknowledging to yourself how you're feeling, and you'll still experience the regulatory benefit. As you silently acknowledge your feelings, you allow yourself to move toward these feelings, staying connected to yourself in the midst of the intensity of the hypo-aroused response.

Sometimes when I'm told I'm alive again, I'll quickly say something about what being dead was like so that the child knows I understand the experience. I might say something like, "That was so hard. I felt so sad and helpless." Whatever the authentic experience was for me is, it's important to say it.

YOU STILL HAVE A MIND!

You'll notice that while lying there dead, your mind will start to wander. You may plan your grocery-shopping list or think about anything that gets your mind's attention and keeps you from feeling what's happening in the room. This is a natural experience and it will happen. You may also feel sleepy or want to zone out. When this occurs, simply notice it and come back to yourself by turning your attention to your body and your breath. If you've managed to die with your eyes open or someplace where you can peek, become aware of what's happening in the room. Become aware of the child.

You might be wondering why it's important to go to such great lengths to manage the hypo-aroused state you're in, and the answer is, *"because the child can feel you."*

After a short but intense sword fight, Lily stabbed me in the heart and announced my death. Luckily, I had been able to fall into a fetal position facing the play, so I could peek out under my arm to track where she was in the room. As I lay there feeling completely unimportant and sad, I used mindfulness and my breath to be with my experience and stay connected to myself. As I did this, I noticed that I was also able to stay connected to Lily. For the next twenty-five minutes, Lily wandered around the room seeming a bit lost, but she eventually made her way to the sand tray and quietly felt the sand and put it into containers. She never looked in my direction or came over to me. Ten more minutes passed and I noticed that it was getting harder for me to remain present with myself. Then my mind decided to completely wander as I began to think about my day and what I was going to do that evening. I disconnected from myself and let go of the energetic container I was holding for Lily. I was no longer present. The moment this happened, Lily stood up from the sand tray and walked straight over to me and kicked me. She'd felt me leave her.

STAYING PRESENT WHILE DEAD

Let me be really honest. It's hard to stay present during hypo-aroused energy. The consensus from my students and my own personal experience is that navigating the waters of hypo-arousal is much harder than navigating hyper-arousal. It takes work and dedication to be with yourself when you're being ignored, dismissed, abandoned and left to die in the play. For most play therapists, this experience brings up all kinds of uncomfortable emotions.

You might be wondering, "If you can't talk and can't move, how are you teaching regulation to a child by lying there?" Even though it may seem as if nothing is happening, much is occurring. When you're lying there mindfully regulating, you're affecting the energy in the room. You're holding the container that allows the child to move toward his uncomfortable feelings and sensations rather than avoid them. In the silence, the child has the opportunity to feel his feelings that are connected to the play.

One of the strategies I use for helping me stay present during this kind of play is visualization. As I feel myself getting smaller and wanting to disappear or disengage, I imagine myself energetically getting as big as the room. I imagine this until energetically I feel bigger than the room and feel myself holding everything in it, including the child.

Reflection: Lie on the floor in the fetal position. You can practice the "death position" if you'd like. Now imagine yourself energetically expanding like a balloon, reaching out to the walls and up to the ceiling, filling every space possible in the room. Feel yourself getting bigger. Feel your presence in the room expand.

REPEATED DEATH

Sometimes a child will kill you multiple times in a session. You die and then you're told to come alive again only to be faced with another death. This type of play can be exhausting and requires a high level of regulation as your own nervous system will be flip-flopping between intense states of hyper-arousal and hypo-arousal. The setup in this play can create feelings of just wanting to die and to stay dead. These feeling are the symbolic representation of the hypo-arousal nervous system wanting to check out and numb out for an extended period of time. It can also create feelings of helplessness and hopelessness, as therapists know that when they're alive in the play, their death is imminent. Over time, it can also create feelings of anger as therapists reach the "enough is enough" point but are unable to do anything about it. Remember, your authentic response and your ability to model regulation through this are key.

DESCRIBING HYPO-AROUSAL

I'm sitting in front of nine-year-old Bobby as he lines up the army men on the floor. The energy in the room is very still. Everything seems to be happening in slow motion. My brain begins to tell me that a fight is going to happen, but I can't feel the anxiety. In fact, I can't feel much of anything. As I watch him set up the army men, I start to feel a little sleepy. When he's finished with the setup, Bobby picks up a soldier and in slow motion moves it to shoot another soldier. He makes a quiet gunshot sound. The sound drifts off, fading away. He picks up a different soldier and again slowly and quietly attacks another soldier. The war has begun, and although I can see it, I can't feel it.

As we're set up to watch play that involves death, we might

also be set up to feel hypo-aroused. When this happens, we can get sleepy, feel numb, spacey and bored and have a hard time registering feelings in our bodies. This is also true when we've been in intense play for a period of time and our nervous system just wants to shut down, as in the case with repeated death. It registers in the brain as too much, and a hypo-aroused response sets in.

You've already learned how to regulate through these intense states using mindfulness, movement, breath and naming your experience out loud, but finding the words when you can't tell what you're experiencing can be challenging. *Describing your experience of feeling hypo-aroused often involves describing the absence of sensations and emotions.* For example, in Bobby's play, I said things like "As I am watching you set up the army men, I can't feel anything in my body. My brain is telling me to be scared because there is a fight happening in front of me, but I just can't feel it." The reason this is significant is that the experience of observing something challenging and not being able to feel it can be very much a part of a trauma response. The body will do whatever it needs to do to manage the intensity it's experiencing. For many children who have experienced or observed trauma, it will be important for them to explore these states of the nervous system as they work toward re-patterning the experiences.

NEGATIVE SELF-TALK

Therapists who have had sessions filled with hypo-arousal often ask me questions like, "What am I doing wrong? What am I missing?" They aren't missing anything. In fact, those thoughts are exactly what they're set up to ask. Negative self-talk is the corresponding brain chatter associated with hypo-arousal. It's also part of the setup. When we're having a hypo-aroused response, it's easy to question ourselves, think we're not understanding something and believe there's something wrong with us. We forget that this is all part of the setup and is most likely what the child is experiencing inside. The trick is to find ways to bring these thoughts into the play so that the child sees us being authentic and attempting to regulate through it.

If the idea of exploring death in the playroom is a challenging thought for you, keep in mind that kids have been playing dead throughout recorded history in every culture. It's normal for children to be curious about the death process. Children are surrounded by death and endings every day. The playroom is the perfect place to explore the emotions and sensations that arise as they process this important part of the life experience.

CHAPTER 9 KEY POINTS

- With death as the symbolic representation in play of the hypo-aroused state of the nervous system, it is a very important state to explore.

- Death can also be used as part of the setup to let us know what it feels like to be helpless, unimportant and deeply rejected and even want to just disappear.

- Death play may be literal for some children who witnessed a death or experienced the loss of a loved one.

- Therapists are often afraid that if we play dead or allow death to occur, we're promoting scary behavior outside the playroom.

- Our ability to remain present, regulate and model mindfulness in the midst of the intensity helps promote integration for the child.

- It's important to die in a way that protects you from being hurt and allows you to maintain knowledge of what's happening in the room with the child.

- Dead people don't talk.

- Even if you're dead, it's important to track time and set boundaries if you need them.

- Playing dead can be just as intense as aggressive play, if not more so.

- When we're dead in the play, regulation is an internal process. By silently acknowledging our feelings, we allow ourselves to move toward these feelings, staying connected to ourselves in the midst of the intensity of the hypo-aroused response.

- Even when we're dead, the child feels our presence.

- It takes work and dedication to be with ourselves when we're being ignored, dismissed, abandoned and left to die in the play. For most play therapists, this experience brings up all kinds of uncomfortable emotions.

- When we're lying there mindfully regulating, we're affecting the energy in the room. We're holding the container that allows the child to move toward his uncomfortable feelings and sensations rather than avoid them. In the silence, the child has the opportunity to feel his feelings that are connected to the play.

- As we're set up to watch play that involves death, we may also be set up to feel hypo-aroused. Describing our experience of feeling hypo-aroused often involves describing the absence of sensations and emotions.

- For many children who have experienced or observed trauma, it's important to explore death from the standpoint of their nervous systems as they work toward re-patterning the experience.

- Negative self-talk is the corresponding brain chatter associated with hypo-arousal. It's also part of the setup.

CLOSING NOTE

I t was my goal to write a book that offered knowledge as well as inspired you to embrace your authenticity. I have witnessed time and again the magic that occurs when therapists allow themselves to fully show up in the playroom while modeling self-regulation and a deep connection to self. It is my belief that it is the moments when we transcend our "shoulds" that we allow ourselves to be guided by a deeper wisdom.

As you move away and avoid your emotions and sensations, you will lose yourself and your center. I want to give you permission to move toward anger, aggression and other intense emotions. Embrace them and move toward them. Learn how to dance with them so that you can transform their energy and birth new possibility for yourself and your clients. Transcend your limiting beliefs regarding aggressive and death energy so that you can awaken your certainty and presence.

It is in this space that deep healing has a chance to occur for our clients and for ourselves. It is my hope that this book provided you with tools to help you navigate death and aggressive play. I also hope that somewhere in this book you found hope and new possibility.

I also want to remind you to be kind to yourself on this journey. You are the most important toy in the playroom.

About the Author

LISA DION, LPC, RPT-S, is an innovative and inspiring teacher and pioneer in play therapy. She is the founder and Executive Director of the Play Therapy Institute of Colorado and creator of "Synergetic Play Therapy," a new model of play therapy bridging the gap between neuroscience and psychology. Lisa teaches and supervises globally, helping transform the lives of thousands of therapists and children. She is the only person in the world who is a Senior Certified Demartini Method Facilitator® and a Registered Play Therapy Supervisor.

Her training and understanding of how the mind and a person's biology drives human behavior allows her to offer her child and adult clients a unique perspective and understanding on how to maximize their potential and develop a greater appreciation for themselves and the people in their lives. Lisa is dedicated to advancing the play therapy field worldwide and is the recipient of the Association for Play Therapy's 2014 Professional Education and Training Award.

For more information, please visit the following websites:

Lisa Dion | *lisa-dion.com*

Synergetic Play Therapy | *synergeticplaytherapy.com*

The Play Therapy Institute of Colorado
playtherapycolorado.com

Printed in Great Britain
by Amazon